# PRAISE FOR DAVID HINTON

"[Hinton] is a national treasure."

— New York Sun

"David Hinton is the best English-language translator of classic Chinese poetry we have, and have had for decades. The translations read in English as though they were written in it originally. A magician's grace glows through all of the poems, a grace and ease uncommonly found, uncommonly masterful."

— *from the citation for the Thornton Wilder Lifetime Achievement Prize, American Academy of Arts and Letters*

"A unique and dazzling achievement."

— *Anne Waldman*

"Hinton's music is subtle, modulated. . . . He continues to enlarge our literary horizon."

— *Rosemary Waldrop, from the citation for the Landon Prize, Academy of American Poets*

"Given the magnitude of his ability and his overall project, Hinton is creating nothing less than a new literary tradition in English."

— *Bei Dao, author of* At the Sky's Edge *and* The Rose of Time

*The*

# WILDS *of* POETRY

## Adventures in Mind and Landscape

## David Hinton

SHAMBHALA
*Boulder*
2017

Shambhala Publications, Inc.
4720 Walnut Street
Boulder, Colorado 80301
www.shambhala.com

9 8 7 6 5 4 3 2 1

FIRST EDITION
*Printed in the United States of America*

⊗ This edition is printed on acid-free paper that meets the
American National Standards Institute z39.48 Standard.
♻ This book is printed on 30% postconsumer recycled paper.
For more information please visit www.shambhala.com.

Distributed in the United States by Penguin Random House LLC
and in Canada by Random House of Canada Ltd

*Designed by Steve Dyer*

LIBRARY OF CONGRESS CATALOGING-IN-PUBLICATION DATA
Names: Hinton, David, 1954– author.
Title: The wilds of poetry: adventures in mind and landscape / David Hinton.
Description: First edition. | Boulder: Shambhala, 2017.
Identifiers: LCCN 2016049367 | ISBN 9781611804607 (paperback)
Subjects: LCSH: American poetry—History and criticism. | Philosophy in
literature. | Consciousness in literature. | Philosophy—East Asia—Influence. |
BISAC: POETRY / American / General. | LITERARY CRITICISM / Poetry. |
LITERARY CRITICISM / American / General.
Classification: LCC PS310.P46 H56 2017 | DDC 811.009/38—dc23
LC record available at https://lccn.loc.gov/2016049367

# Contents

*These Very Wilds*
1

*Procreant Wilds*
Walt Whitman (1819–1892)
15

*China Wilds*
Ezra Pound (1885–1972)
25

*Local Wilds*
William Carlos Williams (1883–1963)
39

*Coastal Wilds*
Robinson Jeffers (1887–1962)
57

*Mountain Wilds*
Kenneth Rexroth (1905–1982)
75

*Mind Wilds*
Charles Olson (1910–1970)
91

*No-Mind Wilds*
John Cage (1912–1992)
117

*Wild Wilds*
Gary Snyder (1930–)
135

*Mammal Wilds*
Michael McClure (1932–)
157

*Primal Wilds*
Jerome Rothenberg (1931–)
179

*Nameless Wilds*
W. S. Merwin (1927–)
203

*Meaningless Wilds*
A. R. Ammons (1926–2001)
221

*Contact Wilds*
Larry Eigner (1927–1996)
241

*Mosaic Wilds*
Ronald Johnson (1935–1998)
263

*Origin Wilds*
Gustaf Sobin (1935–2005)
285

*Itself Wilds*
311

*Credits*
318

*The Wilds of Poetry*

Talk of mysteries!—Think of our life in nature,—daily to be shown matter, to come in contact with it,—rocks, trees, wind on our cheeks! The *solid* earth! The *actual* world! The *common sense*! *Contact*! *Contact*! *Who* are we? *Where* are we?

H. D. Thoreau

# These Very Wilds

IDWAY IN HIS TWO-YEAR STAY AT WALDEN POND
(1845–47), a period of solitary reflection on the nature of
things, of *who* and *where* we are, Thoreau set out on a grueling two-week
journey to the summit of Mount Ktaadn in Maine.* Far from the relatively
tame and domestic environs of Walden Pond, it was a challenging and dis-
orienting journey into extremely remote wilderness. Indeed, the mountain
was so remote that only a few white people had ever climbed it. After more
than a week of travel by boat and foot through increasingly wild territory,
he and his friends arrived at the mountain. Thoreau made two attempts to
climb the peak and failed because the mountain was smothered in wind-
blown cloud, though it almost seems he found the raw wildness of the
place as daunting and impassable as the billowing cloud-cover.

It was on the descent that Thoreau's experience of existential *contact*
occurred: a moment where all the explanations and assumptions fell away,
and he was confronted with the inexplicable thusness of things, this im-
mediate reality, unknowable and unsayable, reality that is pure question,
pure mystery. We can imagine Thoreau's state of mind. His perceptual ex-
perience on the mountain had been intense and bewildering: following a
tumbling torrent of water, he had struggled up steep and tumultuous rock

---

* This journey is recorded in the "Ktaadn" section of Thoreau's *The Maine Woods*.

tangled with strange weather-stunted vegetation, the broken rocks seem-
ingly coming to life (as he says); on a flat shoulder below the summit, he
had crawled across the top of a dense and gnarled expanse of black spruce,
krummholz that he occasionally slumped through or gazed down through
seeing bears in their dens; and looking out from the mountain, views had
been largely reduced to the whites and grays of windblown mist and cloud
("hostile ranks of clouds"), but had occasionally opened to vistas of moun-
tain and surrounding landscape that were in turn quickly erased. All of this
made his reason "dispersed and shadowy, more thin and subtle, like the
air" as he faced "vast, Titanic, inhuman Nature," and it was "more lone
than you can imagine." Thoreau had failed in his mission and was now de-
scending with no further goal, which would have left him open to absorb
unexpected implications of his disorienting experience on the mountain.
The physical difficulty of the journey was continuing, the cumulative ex-
haustion building. This all led somehow to an intensification of Thoreau's
encounter with the Ktaadn wildness he described as "primeval, untamed,
and forever untamable *Nature*, or whatever else men call it . . . pure Na-
ture . . . vast and drear and inhuman."

How powerful questions can be. They can suggest so much more than
is known at the time they are asked, for if there were an adequate answer
they would not be posed. They are therefore wiser than answers, and they
point the way forward. Answers settle things, end movement, but questions
open the possibility of something more, something to come. Thoreau's
questions about *who we are* and *where we are* do all of this for his moment
in Western intellectual history, and they encapsulate the philosophical in-
quiry driving the central thread of innovative poetry in twentieth-century
America, the subject of this book. They are the most profound questions
possible, really, for at their deepest level they allow no answer. They
simply pose the unsayable reality of *contact*, which is all question and all
mystery—a moment in which the mind's orienting certainties fail, even
the certainty of self-identity, leaving one open to the experience of sheer
immediacy. It is the experience of a mind perfectly emptied of all content,
all the received explanations and assumptions about *who we are* and *where
we are*; and so, a mind open to the fundamental reality of the material
Cosmos in and of itself, open therefore to *these very wilds* we inhabit day
by day, however rarely we are aware of that existential level of immediacy.

That experience itself is absolute. As soon as we try to explain, it is lost, because explanation involves language and concepts, the human structures that preclude wholesale *contact*. Thoreau's foundational questions are in fact rhetorical questions that actually say: *there is no knowing who and where we are*. And it's true, there is no knowing at this level. Nevertheless, those questions can be taken as a starting point, and they distill the central issue in nineteenth- and twentieth-century intellectual history: What is the self? What is the Cosmos? And what is the interrelation between them? They were crucial questions because science and common sense had rendered the culture's traditional answers no longer tenable.

Those answers, handed down from Greek and Judeo-Christian philosophy, went something like this: We are souls, made from spirit-stuff fundamentally different from the material world we inhabit. This transcendental soul is the center of abstract rational thought; it is immortal; and it is a visitor on this planet, a kind of alien whose true home is in some heavenly sphere, dwelling-place of God, who created both the spirit-realm of souls and the material realm of the empirical universe. The implications of this scheme are manifold, but they all devalue the physical earth and our relation to it. Abstract "truth" is valued over immediate experience. Rational mind is valued over body, which is considered impure and evil. The earth is considered nothing more than a resource base for human use, and additionally, as a proving ground, the backdrop for our human drama of eternal salvation or damnation. Thoreau witnessed in the early days of his Ktaadn journey the menacing impact this clutch of beliefs has on the world, for he spent those days traveling through the wastage of clear-cut logging that was destroying the primeval Maine woods. While native cultures had inhabited those woods for ten thousand years and left the ecosystem intact, white colonizers devastated the ecosystem in a matter of decades.

Enlightenment science was showing how false those traditional assumptions were, which left the field open for answers that were more empirically valid than the traditional ones. By the time of Thoreau's *contact*, the traditional cosmology had long since been replaced in intellectual history by various kinds of post-Christian/scientific pantheism—most notably Deism, which had been the prevailing conceptual framework among America's intellectuals for over a century, including America's Founding Fathers. Deism considered art and science to be the true religion, because those practices engaged us with the immediate reality of the Cosmos, and that reality was itself the divine. Closely related to Deism's scientific pantheism were various versions of pantheism among Romantic poets and painters, for whom the natural world evoked a profound sense of awe, awe they could only explain as a kind of religious experience.

A realm that is beautiful and spiritual, sustaining and transforming—we take for granted these attitudes toward the wild, but they were all but unknown in the West prior to the Deists and Romantics. Instead, the wild was generally seen as loathsome and hideous, fearsome and threatening, desolate and evil and devilish. Hence, Romantic and Deist thought represents a transformation in our relationship to the natural world so profound it is difficult now to imagine it. At the outset, pantheism was necessary to invest the wild with an aura of the divine, thereby explaining that Romantic feeling of awe or wonder or the sublime, but eventually that began to change in the work of the naturalist and explorer Alexander von Humboldt, and following him, Thoreau and Whitman.

Humboldt was an international superstar, and his hugely influential science dispensed with God or the divine and proposed that romantic awe in the face of sublime wilderness derives from our "communion with nature" as a magisterial presence, "a unity in diversity of phenomena; a harmony, blending together all created things, however dissimilar in form and attributes; one great whole animated by the breath of life." Here he means *breath* not in the sense of some divine agency, but as a single unifying life-force inherent to the material Cosmos, for he elsewhere describes the Cosmos as "animated by one breath" and "animated by internal forces." Humboldt described earth as an organic whole, a living web of interrelated life: a "net-like intricate fabric," a "wonderful web of organic life." In this he essentially invented the idea of "nature" as we now know it.

No less important in terms of intellectual history, he confirmed romantic intimations that the human mind is woven into the material web of life:

> External nature may be opposed to the intellectual world, as if the latter were not comprised within the limits of the former, or nature may be opposed to art when the latter is defined as a manifestation of the intellectual power of man; but these contrasts, which we find reflected in the most cultivated languages, must not lead us to separate the sphere of nature from that of mind. . . .

Standard pantheism leaves the human out of divine nature, as soul, but the powerful inner experience Humboldt and the Romantics found in the presence of nature (communion, awe, the sublime, etc.) suggested otherwise, suggested for the first time in a broadly influential statement that consciousness is integral to the material Cosmos.

Humboldt's revolutionary ideas appeared not only in the form of conceptual propositions but also in the form of widely read books, which combined scientific information with poetic descriptions of landscape to form an emotional fabric of communion between the human and the wild. This combination (which we now call "nature writing") was transformative for Thoreau, making him into the writer we know, and for Whitman, who kept Humboldt's books on his desk as he wrote "Song of Myself" (see p. 18). And they turn out to be the very ideas this book will follow through twentieth-century poetry, where they are accessible not simply as ideas, but as immediate poetic experience.

It is in the midst of this transformation in intellectual history, just prior to encountering Humboldt, that Thoreau found himself on Mount Ktaadn with all explanations (old and new) gone, experiencing *contact*. As that *contact* returns us to a place before the structures of mind, it is an experience of an original nature of consciousness prior to its separation from the world as alien soul: consciousness in its primitive openness, before writing and ideas and religions started closing us in on ourselves, separating us out as centers of identity somehow disconnected from all of that *other*. In this openness, *who we are* is woven into *where we are*, and consciousness moves with the same patterns and rhythms as everything else—the seasons and winds, mountains and stars.

The philosophical transformation from a spiritualist to an empiricist worldview remained central to philosophical and scientific endeavor, culminating philosophically in the existentialists (as the name suggests), especially in the radical phenomenology/ontology of Husserl ("Back to the things themselves"), Heidegger, and Merleau-Ponty. But this transformation has perhaps found its most radical manifestation in modern American poetry, whose central task over the last century has been to rediscover that primal nature of consciousness, to reimagine consciousness not as a spirit-center with its abstract process of self-enclosed thought, but as an openness to immediate experience—as, indeed, a site where the Cosmos is open to itself. For it is in that immediate experience that *who we are* is woven into *where we are*. In this, the twentieth-century American avant-garde has been a philosophical/spiritual endeavor, reinventing that form of consciousness as actual lived experience rather than the kind of abstract ideas that philosophy and science offer.

Between 3,000 and 2,500 years ago, ancient China underwent a cultural transformation very similar to that of the modern West: the transformation from a spiritualist to an empiricist worldview, which entailed a rediscovery of consciousness in its original nature as woven into the tissue of existence.* And as we will see, modern American poetry's reinvention of consciousness was a reformulation of the insights that emerged from that cultural transformation in ancient China and eventually migrated to America beginning in the early years of the twentieth century—insights embodied in Taoist and Ch'an (Japanese: Zen) Buddhist thought, the arts, and the classical Chinese language itself.

The historical beginnings of Chinese civilization lie in the Shang Dynasty (1766–1040 B.C.E.), during which it was believed that all things were created and controlled by Shang Ti ("Celestial Lord"), an all-powerful monotheistic deity very like the Judeo-Christian God. As high ancestor of the Shang rulers, Shang Ti provided those rulers with a transcendental source of legitimacy through lineage. Indeed, it gave them supernatural power because they could, through prayer and ritual, influence Shang Ti's shaping of events. All aspects of people's lives were thus controlled by the emperor: weather, harvest, politics, economics, religion, etc. Indeed, as in the traditional West, people didn't experience themselves as substantially different from spirits, for the human realm was simply an extension of the spirit realm.

Eventually, the Shang emperors grew tyrannical, and the dynasty was overthrown by the Chou Dynasty (1040–223 B.C.E.), whereupon the Chou rulers reinvented Shang Ti as an impersonal "heaven," thus ending the Shang's claim to legitimacy by lineage. The Chou rulers justified their rule by claiming they had the "Mandate of Heaven," so when their rule was in turn challenged, the last semblance of this theocratic cosmology crumbled, leaving no organizing system to structure society. Philosophers like Lao Tzu and Confucius (c. fifth to sixth centuries B.C.E.) struggled to invent a new philosophical system that could replace the spiritualistic system with a humanistic one based on empirical reality. One aspect of

------

* For a more detailed description of this process, see the introduction to my translation of the *Tao Te Ching* (Counterpoint, 2015).

this transformation was the reinvention of heaven as an entirely empirical phenomenon: it became the generative cosmological principle that drives change, thereby secularizing the sacred while at the same time investing the secular with sacred dimensions. Here, China had invented something akin to the pantheism that appeared 2,500 years later in the West's Deism and Romanticism.

This transition moment was soon superseded by an entirely secular concept: Tao (道), which was essentially synonymous with "heaven," but without the metaphysical stretch. *Tao* is the central concept in Taoism as formulated in Lao Tzu's *Tao Te Ching*, a poetic text that is the seminal work in Chinese spiritual philosophy. *Tao* means most literally "Way," as in a road or pathway, but Lao Tzu uses it to describe the empirical Cosmos as a single living tissue that is inexplicably generative in its very nature. As such it is an ongoing cosmological process, an ontological path*Way* by which things come into existence, evolve through their lives, and then go out of existence, only to be transformed and reemerge in a new form. Our belonging to this magical tissue made the world of our immediate experience wholly mysterious and wondrous and sufficient in and of itself. There was no need for the "sacred" or "divine." So while much of the West saw the natural world as godless evil even into modern times, China has a three-thousand-year engagement with the wild as spiritually sustaining. And over those millennia, Chinese culture developed a philosophical and artistic tradition founded on the wild—a tradition that, again, transformed modern American poetry and the possibilities of experience that poetry helped to open.

Lao Tzu's vision apparently derives from a primal oral tradition that persisted outside the mythological power structures of the Shang and Chou dynasties, for it represents a return to the earliest levels of proto-Chinese culture: to the Paleolithic, it seems, where the empirical Cosmos was recognized as female in its fundamental nature, as a magisterial and perpetually generative organism in constant transformation. In fact, Lao Tzu often refers to Tao as *female* or *mother*. This is the root of a remarkable fact: high Chinese civilization, for all its complexity and sophistication, never forgot its origins in the primitive. The primitive was the very thing responsible for the distinctive nature of its complexity and sophistication. Indeed, for the artistic-intellectual tradition that followed Lao Tzu, sage wisdom involved dwelling as an integral part of Tao's generative cosmological process. This involved practices of philosophical and artistic self-cultivation supported by a number of key concepts that became central in America's modern poetic avant-garde.

In his attempts to explain Tao, Lao Tzu deployed the concept of *tzu-jan* (自然). The literal meaning of *tzu-jan* is "self" + "thus," from which comes "self-so" or "the of-itself," which leads to a more descriptive translation, "occurrence appearing of itself," for *tzu-jan* is meant to describe the ten thousand things emerging spontaneously from the generative source, each according to its own nature, independent and self-sufficient, then eventually dying and returning to that source, only to reappear transformed into other self-generating forms. That source is Tao, reality seen at the deep ontological level as a single tissue rather than as ten thousand individual things. And so, *tzu-jan* emphasizes the *thusness* of individual things, the ten thousand things as we can know them in attentive immediate experience. Tao is reality seen as a single tissue; *tzu-jan* is that same reality seen as an assemblage of individual forms. This *tzu-jan* cosmology entails a different, more primal sense of time that we will see enacted in some of the avant-garde poets: rather than the linear time of the West, time as a kind of metaphysical river flowing past, it is nothing other than the movement of change itself, an ongoing generative moment in which things emerge from and return to the generative ontological tissue.

A closely related concept is *wu-wei* (無為), which means "not acting" in the sense of acting without the metaphysics of self, or of being absent when you act. This selfless action is the movement of *tzu-jan*, so *wu-wei* means acting as an integral part of *tzu-jan*'s spontaneous process. It was a spiritual discipline that ancient Chinese artist-intellectuals pursued in their daily lives and in their artistic practices. Tao, *tzu-jan*, *wu-wei*: these terms provide a concise framework through which to understand the poetic thought of innovative modern American poets. Even if poets often didn't use this terminology, the concepts were foundational, and, as we will see, they came from China through a complex process of cultural translation.

Lao Tzu's insights were eventually honed into a formalized spiritual practice in Ch'an (Japanese: Zen) Buddhism. After it took shape around 400 C.E., virtually all artist-intellectuals in ancient China practiced Ch'an as a form of Taoist thought that was refined and reconfigured by the arrival of Buddhism from India, and artistic practice (poetry, painting, calligraphy) was considered Taoist/Ch'an spiritual practice. Even more than Taoist thought, Ch'an was a fundamental transformative influence in the

American poetic avant-garde, and in all of the arts in post–World War II America.

There are two aspects of Ch'an practice. One is koan practice, wherein students are asked to resolve insoluble puzzles as a way to break down conventional structures of thought, to see through our stories and explanations about the world and so return to *contact*, to our original nature as consciousness in the open. Solutions to such koans always involve responding with a spontaneous immediacy that lies outside any logical analysis; and in koan training, the teacher may push the student toward that goal with enigmatic utterances and outbursts and antics. The correct answer to a koan is whatever emerges spontaneously from that primal silence and emptiness where the logical construction of thoughts has not yet begun. The difficulty is learning how to inhabit that place. That goal was widely shared in various ways by much of the twentieth-century American avant-garde, and it engendered a frequent use of koan-like strategies to get at those deep levels of consciousness.

The other aspect of Ch'an practice is meditation, Ch'an's primary means of fathoming reality at the more primal level that lies beyond words and concepts, which also means moving past that illusory separation between consciousness and Cosmos. Meditation was also widely practiced among postwar avant-garde poets, and in its barest outlines it involves sitting quietly and watching thoughts come and go in a field of silent emptiness. From this attention to thought's movement comes meditation's first revelation: that we are, as a matter of observable fact, separate from our thoughts and memories. That is, we are not the center of identity we assume ourselves to be in our day-to-day lives—that center reified as a soul in Christian mythology, and surviving in our post-Christian world as a center of abstract thought that takes the empirical realm as the object of its contemplation, thus defining us as fundamentally outside that realm. Instead, we are the empty awareness (known in Ch'an terminology as "empty mind") that watches identity rehearsing itself in thoughts and memories relentlessly coming and going.

Eventually the stream of thought falls silent, and you inhabit empty mind, free of that center of identity—free, that is, of the self-absorbed and relentless process of thought that precludes *contact* in our day-to-day experience. And so, you inhabit the most fundamental nature of consciousness, the dark and empty awareness that is nothing other than the Cosmos looking out at itself. It is here that you inhabit the full depth of immediate experience, of *contact*, for here all assumptions and explanations have fallen away, leaving consciousness in the open. In this empty mind, the act of perception becomes a spiritual practice in which the opening of consciousness is a mirror allowing no distinction between inside and outside. Identity becomes whatever sight fills eye and mind, becomes all of existence itself. This is simply a deep description of everyday mindfulness, that attentiveness to things at hand that enables us to inhabit our lives with all immediacy as a rich and profound experience.

So the end result of Ch'an practice is an awakening in which all our structures of understanding fall away and consciousness is left wide open to all the depths of immediate experience, exactly what Thoreau encountered on Mount Ktaadn. This was a familiar and desirable experience for the artist-intellectuals of ancient China: the heart of spiritual practice, a way to see the Cosmos whole, to dwell as an integral part of Tao, and thereby establish a deeper everyday experience of life. Philosophically, it is what we would now call "deep ecology," a reweaving of consciousness and landscape, planet, Cosmos. But in Thoreau's West it was not so familiar; and indeed, it was quite terrifying, a terror that continued in the philosophical tradition as existential angst, nausea, etc. While thinkers like Thoreau felt utterly lost when their fundamental assumptions vanished, the experience was reassuring for the ancient Chinese, renewing a sense of belonging to Tao, that numinous generative tissue, and it led to a poetic tradition in which *contact* is the fabric from which poems are made:

## AT HSIEH COVE

The ox path I'm on ends in a rabbit trail, and suddenly
I'm facing open plains and empty sky on all four sides.

My thoughts follow white egrets—a pair taking flight,
leading sight across a million blue mountains rising

ridge beyond ridge, my gaze lingering near then far,
enthralled by peaks crowded together or there alone.

Even a hill or valley means thoughts beyond knowing—
and all this? A crusty old man's now a wide-eyed child!

*Yang Wan-li, 1127–1206 C.E.*

EVENING VIEW

Already at South Tower: evening stillness.
In the darkness, a few forest birds astir.

The bustling city-wall sinks out of sight —
deeper, deeper. Just four mountain peaks.

*Wei Ying-wu, c. 737–792 C.E.*

The difference is that the West had not yet completed that transition from otherworldly monotheism to secular spirituality — a fact witnessed in Thoreau's fearful question itself, with its *who*, which implicitly assumes the otherworldly soul that Thoreau inherited from the Western tradition. It seems clear now that the question would more accurately be: *What are we?*

It is striking how closely this transition in the West follows the outlines of the transition in ancient China. Just as *heaven* came to mean something like "natural process" in China as a way of making empirical reality "divine," Deist and Romantic pantheism invested our everyday world with mystery and wonder by calling it "God." Just as Taoism's sense of the Cosmos as a generative tissue appears to have survived outside of the power structures of Shang monotheism, survived from perhaps Paleolithic levels of Chinese culture, the West's pantheism too grew from an alternative tradition that survived outside of the power structures: from Spinoza to Lucretius and back to the pre-Socratics Epicurus and Heraclitus, who represent the earliest emergence from a more primal preliterate intellectual framework. (As we will see, the modern avant-garde had a sustained interest in returning consciousness to the primitive.) And just as China secularized this sacralized reality in Tao, the West secularized it in the Cosmos as known by modern science, which is also (though how often is it described this way?) essentially female: an organic and harmonious system that is a tissue of perpetually self-generating transformation.

This transition became the engine driving literary innovation: the British Romantic poets, Emerson and Thoreau and Whitman. But Thoreau's experience on Ktaadn signals a further step in the transformation from a spiritualist to an empiricist conceptual framework. Thoreau didn't have the tools to understand what happened to him, what he was seeing, so it was all question and wonder, but the ancient Chinese did have the tools, and it was for them an *awakening*, a moment in which the ongoing process of self-absorbed thought and all the explanatory structures of the mind fail, leaving you open to the experience of unmediated immediacy: *contact*. And that immediacy was for them the spiritual experience of belonging profoundly to empirical reality as pure wonder and mystery. The goal of spiritual practice in ancient China was to make that awakening the form of everyday experience, and Thoreau's later *Journals* (see p. 119, 267) indicate Thoreau shared that practice in some sense, for in them Thoreau's self-expression is increasingly descriptive: the world itself, as if he found more and more over his life that mirror-deep identity the Chinese ancients cultivated.

Poetry is most deeply a way of doing philosophy—not as mere juggling of abstractions, but as lived and felt experience. This is how the twentieth-century avant-garde used it, as a way to construct and inhabit a worldview. Ancient Chinese thought is a crucial influence driving the innovations of that tradition—and it makes perfect sense, for the Taoist/Ch'an conceptual framework represented a fuller and more coherent account of the radical insights that were ripe for realization in the West. And like China's ancient artist-intellectuals, that avant-garde took *contact* as its central concern, certain that only in empirical immediacy was it possible to achieve authenticity in living, and clarity in *who* and *where we are*.

*Contact*, the primacy of the immediate: it is not such a difficult idea, but in terms of actual experience, the stuff of life and poetry, it is a difficult lesson we must learn over and over. *Contact* itself is unsayable precisely because it lies outside all concepts, but these poets, each in their own way, guide us to the experience of *contact*. They show us new ways of being alive to the world in the tangible here and now. And from that beginning point, they explore the implications of that elemental experience, most importantly a different sense of self-identity: Thoreau's *who we are*. This line of poetic thought represents a lived form of deep ecology, the "rewilding" of consciousness. It involves ways of knowing ourselves outside of received Western assumptions; and so, not surprisingly, it is often informed by other cultures, especially ancient Chinese and primal cultures. Hence, the poets in this innovative tradition establish consciousness as wild each in their own way, together creating their own wilderness: "the wilds of poetry."

Central to this for most poets is the way they push language into wild forms in various ways: organic and open-field, breath-driven, text interspersed with fields of open space/silence, fragmentation and collage. Language is the medium of thought, essence of self-identity, so by rewilding language they rewild identity. And it makes sense this rewilding often takes place in the context of wilderness, where the cocoon of human culture is absent and the vastness of the Cosmos is most dramatically and immediately present. As a philosophical instrument, poetry is especially powerful because it can operate in that wilderness, open experience to the silent depths outside of language and thought, reveal areas of consciousness outside our language-centered day-to-day identity. Prose can talk about this, but poetry can enact it through its reshaping of language. It can create wild mind as immediate experience for the reader.

Innovative poetry in twentieth-century America is at heart an ecopoetic tradition, though not in the sense of poetry where "nature" happens to appear, where that traditional Western spirit-center encounters an animal or tree, ocean or mountain. Instead, it is ecopoetic in the deeper sense that it articulates a weave of consciousness and landscape, a deep reexperiencing of consciousness as an integral part of the Cosmos, the wild. Although we live in a post-Christian world, we generally still experience a radical separation between a kind of spirit-center and the world it looks out on, a separation enshrined (to take one small example) in concepts such as *nature* and *wild*, which refer to the world exclusive of human consciousness, thereby defining as a matter of cultural assumption the human as fundamentally different from and outside of empirical reality. Ecopoetry reintegrates human consciousness into landscape and Cosmos, into *nature* and the *wild*. Even if this happens most often in some kind of engagement with wilderness in the broad sense of empirical reality outside of human cultural constructions, it sometimes happens in more human and urban settings, for they too are part of the wild Cosmos. The important thing for ecopoetry is the weaving together of consciousness with landscape, ecosystem, Cosmos—thereby returning it to its original wild nature.

This is primarily a philosophical book, and as such it traces that ecopoetic strand of thought by presenting the voices of its major innovators, those who established the terms for innovative poetic practice. The poets included here are all male, but the interest is to follow their attempts to reimagine the male self, that abstract cerebral "soul" separate from and lording over the earth (part and parcel with a Christian cosmology and domineering male sky-god). These poets try to replace that with a gentler self that dwells as an integral part of the generative, female Cosmos known by modern science—that is, to use the Chinese term, the female *Tao*. Given the line of thought this book explores, it would make perfect sense that women would play a major role in the tradition traced here. That is not the case for the well-rehearsed reason that women were largely excluded from the intellectual and literary world through the years discussed in this book (though soon afterward they began rising quickly in prominence and have now established themselves as an equal or even dominant force in contemporary poetry). However, this book is an attempt to excavate a female dimension in the tradition, to track the discovery that it is the tradition's most powerful and transformative proposition, that it is the impulse driving the tradition and the conceptual source for virtually all innovative poetry in the second half of twentieth-century America.

Shaped by the Taoist/Ch'an conceptual framework, classical Chinese poetry is at heart a "mountains-and-rivers" ("landscape") tradition, an ecopoetic tradition in every sense; and remarkably, the modern American avant-garde can be seen as an extension of that mountains-and-rivers tradition. Because they did not inherit a deep-ecological system of thought, innovative American poets needed to borrow and conjure new ideas as they reinvented poetic language and thought outside of cultural/poetic norms. Their richest borrowing came from ancient China, and it led to exciting new ways of making poetry.

Tracing the development of this ecopoetic tradition is a way not only to understand the weave of consciousness and landscape more deeply, but also to *experience* it more deeply, for that immediate experience is what the poems themselves offer. Hence, this book represents a kind of philosophical method, exploring ideas in the introductions and then letting the poems make those ideas available as immediate poetic experience. As such, the following chapters attempt to present and think through a collage of the work that transformed the possibilities of the poetic tradition and of human consciousness. It is work from a range of poets who each create in their work the experience of consciousness woven into landscape and Cosmos in their own singular and innovative way, each in their own *talk of mysteries*.

# Procreant Wilds

## *Walt Whitman*
## (*1819–1892*)

THIS STORY OF THE INNOVATIVE/ECOPOETIC TRADI-
tion in modern American poetry really begins in the mid-
nineteenth century with Walt Whitman. A few years after Thoreau posed
his existential questions, Whitman began making a poetry from the imme-
diacy of *contact*, and in doing so he pushed the revelations of post-Chris-
tian science, Deism, and Romantic pantheism to new depths. Whitman
too was still caught in the terminology of the Western intellectual tradi-
tion—soul and the pantheist god of Deism—but the actual contours of his
poetic thinking had moved beyond that conceptual framework. Keeping
Humboldt's insights always in mind (see p. 4), Whitman gave them poetic
voice and in fact pushed them to the point that they could most accurately
be described as Taoist.

Whitman speaks always at the level of *contact*, where the distinction be-
tween self and Cosmos has vanished. It is noteworthy that with Whitman,
Thoreau's terror at *contact* has become a sense of belonging or enlighten-
ment (much as it does in ancient China, where it is the very definition of
sage insight), a sense that will continue through the twentieth-century po-
etic tradition. Whitman speaks everywhere and in myriad ways of himself
being integral to things, identifies himself over and over with long catalogs
of things and events, scenes and tales (told in the straightforward language
of his day-job as a journalist). He speaks as the Cosmos itself: the miracle

of empirical reality, immediate and unsayable. "Song of Myself" (1855), his signature poem, begins with the words "I celebrate myself," "celebrate" not only in its familiar sense, but also in its earliest sense of performing a religious ceremony. And as part of this integration of self and Cosmos, Whitman speaks as a body, sexual in its deepest nature. It was a voice all but unprecedented in English. Language is the material of self-identity, and the dominant language of English poetry was that of the soul, its deep rhythms often echoing the King James Bible. It was a privileged language of rhyme and meter, abstract and linear thought, embellishment and arch diction. When Whitman reinvented language as the voice of the body, he reinvented identity as embodied and organic and integral to earth.

Rather than following a linear development of thought, that linear abstract thought of the soul, "Song of Myself" is a collage of juxtaposed fragments: identity as an ecstatic field of simultaneous perception and thought. The poem sprawls with a strange intensity, driven by its own propulsion rather than the artificial constraints of rhyme and meter—an impulse marked by the frequent use of commas to divide sentences, rather than periods that stop the forward movement. It is the voice of a sexual body adrift in the energy flow of the Cosmos, and it is driven by the spontaneous energy of the Cosmos. Most fundamentally, it is mind rewilded, thought moving with the motion of natural process—and so, identity wholly integrated into the Cosmos seen as an ongoing process of transformation.

Whitman recognized that the Cosmos revealed in *contact* is an organic sexual whole in constant transformation, and that each individual being is part of that whole and part of that process of transformation through which one life becomes another by means of death and sex: "Urge and urge and urge, / Always the procreant urge of the world." This procreant Cosmos is by nature generative—and so, female. And Whitman thought experiencing the wild could return us to "the naked source-life of us all—to the breast of the great silent savage all-acceptive Mother." It is a concept that could not survive with its implications in any deep way, given the dominant male-oriented conceptual framework; but as we will see, it emerges as a broader cultural force in modern American poetry. And understood fully as a female cosmology—"source-life" and "savage"—it is nothing other than Lao Tzu's Tao.

All of this is radically innovative in terms of both poetry and philosophy. Whitman's poetry concerns itself not with spiritualized ideas and dramas, nor with poeticized and beautified language. It speaks instead of concrete and immediate reality in his "barbaric yawp" of plain speech. This is the other reason for Whitman's long catalogs: it is his way of celebrating things in and of themselves without distinguishing between beautiful and ugly, poetic and unpoetic, celebrating them because they are all part of the self-sufficient *thusness* of things (Lao Tzu's *tzu-jan*). And his long poems are brawny sprawling affairs ("Song of Myself" runs to 1,336 lines in its original edition), a form that replicates the sprawling plenitude of the Cosmos. Plainspoken, collage-like, organic, propulsive—this form is no less important than what it says, for it embodies the philosophical dimensions he talks about, dimensions that remain central throughout the innovative twentieth-century tradition. It is Whitman's attempt to say the unsayable, the reality of consciousness and Cosmos in all the immediacy of *contact*, where *who we are* is essentially the procreant Cosmos of *where we are*.

*from* SONG OF MYSELF

I celebrate myself,
And what I assume you shall assume,
For every atom belonging to me as good belongs to you.

I loafe and invite my soul,
I lean and loafe at my ease . . . . observing a spear of summer grass.

Houses and rooms are full of perfumes . . . . the shelves are crowded with
    perfumes,
I breathe the fragrance myself, and know it and like it,
The distillation would intoxicate me also, but I shall not let it.

The atmosphere is not a perfume . . . . it has no taste of the distillation . . . .
    it is odorless,
It is for my mouth forever . . . . I am in love with it,
I will go to the bank by the wood and become undisguised and naked,
I am mad for it to be in contact with me.

The smoke of my own breath,
Echos, ripples, and buzzed whispers . . . . loveroot, silkthread, crotch and vine,
My respiration and inspiration . . . . the beating of my heart . . . . the passing
    of blood and air through my lungs,
The sniff of green leaves and dry leaves, and of the shore and darkcolored
    sea-rocks, and of hay in the barn,
The sound of the belched words of my voice . . . . words loosed to the eddies
    of the wind,
A few light kisses . . . . a few embraces . . . . a reaching around of arms,
The play of shine and shade on the trees as the supple boughs wag,
The delight alone or in the rush of the streets, or along the fields and hillsides,
The feeling of health . . . . the full-noon trill . . . . the song of me rising from
    bed and meeting the sun.

Have you reckoned a thousand acres much? Have you reckoned the earth much?
Have you practiced so long to learn to read?
Have you felt so proud to get at the meaning of poems?

Stop this day and night with me and you shall possess the origin of all poems,
You shall possess the good of the earth and sun . . . . there are millions
      of suns left,
You shall no longer take things at second or third hand . . . . nor look through
      the eyes of the dead . . . . nor feed on the spectres in books,
You shall not look through my eyes either, nor take things from me,
You shall listen to all sides and filter them from yourself.

I have heard what the talkers were talking . . . . the talk of the beginning and
      the end,
But I do not talk of the beginning or the end.

There was never any more inception than there is now,
Nor any more youth or age than there is now;
And will never be any more perfection than there is now,
Nor any more heaven or hell than there is now.

Urge and urge and urge,
Always the procreant urge of the world.

Out of the dimness opposite equals advance . . . . Always substance and
      increase,
Always a knit of identity . . . . always distinction . . . . always a breed of life.

To elaborate is no avail . . . . Learned and unlearned feel that it is so.

Sure as the most certain sure . . . . plumb in the uprights, well entretied,
      braced in the beams,
Stout as a horse, affectionate, haughty, electrical,
I and this mystery here we stand.

————————

What do you think has become of the young and old men?
And what do you think has become of the women and children?

They are alive and well somewhere;
The smallest sprout shows there is really no death,

And if ever there was it led forward life, and does not wait at the end to arrest it,
And ceased the moment life appeared.

All goes onward and outward . . . . and nothing collapses,
And to die is different from what any one supposed, and luckier.

Has any one supposed it lucky to be born?
I hasten to inform him or her it is just as lucky to die, and I know it.

---

I am the mate and companion of people, all just as immortal and fathomless
    as myself;
They do not know how immortal, but I know.

---

The pure contralto sings in the organloft,
The carpenter dresses his plank . . . . the tongue of his foreplane whistles its
    wild ascending lisp,
The married and unmarried children ride home to their thanks-giving dinner,
The pilot seizes the king-pin, he heaves down with a strong arm,
The mate stands braced in the whaleboat, lance and harpoon are ready,
The duck-shooter walks by silent and cautious stretches,
The deacons are ordained with crossed hands at the altar,
The spinning-girl retreats and advances to the hum of the big wheel,
The farmer stops by the bars of a Sunday and looks at the oats and rye,
The lunatic is carried at last to the asylum a confirmed case,
He will never sleep any more as he did in the cot in his mother's bedroom;
The jour printer with gray head and gaunt jaws works at his case,
He turns his quid of tobacco, his eyes get blurred with the manuscript;
The malformed limbs are tied to the anatomist's table,
What is removed drops horribly in a pail;
The quadroon girl is sold at the stand . . . . the drunkard nods by the
    barroom stove,
The machinist rolls up his sleeves . . . . the policeman travels his beat . . . .
    the gate-keeper marks who pass,

---

The torches shine in the dark that hangs on the Chattahoochee or Altamahaw;
Patriarchs sit at supper with sons and grandsons and great grandsons around
      them,
In walls of adobie, in canvas tents, rest hunters and trappers after their day's sport.
The city sleeps and the country sleeps,
The living sleep for their time . . . . the dead sleep for their time,
The old husband sleeps by his wife and the young husband sleeps by his wife;
And these one and all tend inward to me, and I tend outward to them,
And such as it is to be of these more or less I am.

I am of old and young, of the foolish as much as the wise,
Regardless of others, ever regardful of others,
Maternal as well as paternal, a child as well as a man,
Stuffed with the stuff that is coarse, and stuffed with the stuff that is fine,

---

Through me many long dumb voices,
Voices of the interminable generations of slaves,
Voices of prostitutes and of deformed persons,
Voices of the diseased and despairing, and of thieves and dwarfs,
Voices of cycles of preparation and accretion,
And of the threads that connect the stars—and of wombs, and of the
      fatherstuff,
And of the rights of them the others are down upon,
Of the trivial and flat and foolish and despised,
Of fog in the air and beetles rolling balls of dung.

---

I dote on myself . . . . there is that lot of me, and all so luscious,
Each moment and whatever happens thrills me with joy.

I cannot tell how my ankles bend . . . . nor whence the cause of my faintest
      wish,
Nor the cause of the friendship I emit . . . . nor the cause of the friendship
      I take again.

To walk up my stoop is unaccountable . . . . I pause to consider if it really be,
That I eat and drink is spectacle enough for the great authors and schools,
A morning-glory at my window satisfies me more than the metaphysics of books.

--------

. . . to feel the puzzle of puzzles,
And that we call Being.

To be in any form, what is that?
If nothing lay more developed the quahaug and its callous shell were enough.

Mine is no callous shell,
I have instant conductors all over me whether I pass or stop,
They seize every object and lead it harmlessly through me.

I merely stir, press, feel with my fingers, and am happy,
To touch my person to some one else's is about as much as I can stand.

Is this then a touch? . . . . quivering me to a new identity,
Flames and ether making a rush for my veins,

--------

I teach straying from me, yet who can stray from me?
I follow you whoever you are from the present hour;
My words itch at your ears till you understand them.

I do not say these things for a dollar, or to fill up the time while I wait for a boat;
It is you talking just as much as myself . . . . I act as the tongue of you,
It was tied in your mouth . . . . in mine it begins to be loosened.

I swear I will never mention love or death inside a house,
And I swear I never will translate myself at all, only to him or her who privately
     stays with me in the open air.

If you would understand me go to the heights or water-shore,
The nearest gnat is an explanation and a drop or the motion of waves a key,
The maul the oar and the handsaw second my words.

There is that in me . . . . I do not know what it is . . . . but I know it is in me.

Wrenched and sweaty . . . . calm and cool then my body becomes;
I sleep . . . . I sleep long.

I do not know it . . . . it is without name . . . . it is a word unsaid,
It is not in any dictionary or utterance or symbol.

Something it swings on more than the earth I swing on,
To it the creation is the friend whose embracing awakes me.

Perhaps I might tell more . . . . Outlines! I plead for my brothers and sisters.

Do you see O my brothers and sisters?
It is not chaos or death . . . . it is form and union and plan . . . . it is eternal
      life . . . . it is happiness.

The past and present wilt . . . . I have filled them and emptied them,
And proceed to fill my next fold of the future.

Listener up there! Here you . . . . what have you to confide to me?
Look in my face while I snuff the sidle of evening,
Talk honestly, for no one else hears you, and I stay only a minute longer.

Do I contradict myself?
Very well then . . . . I contradict myself;
I am large . . . . I contain multitudes.

I concentrate toward them that are nigh . . . . I wait on the door-slab.

Who has done his day's work and will soonest be through with his supper?
Who wishes to walk with me?

Will you speak before I am gone? Will you prove already too late?

The spotted hawk swoops by and accuses me . . . . he complains of my gab
    and my loitering.

I too am not a bit tamed . . . . I too am untranslatable,
I sound my barbaric yawp over the roofs of the world.

The last scud of day holds back for me,
It flings my likeness after the rest and true as any on the shadowed wilds,
It coaxes me to the vapor and the dusk.

I depart as air . . . . I shake my white locks at the runaway sun,
I effuse my flesh in eddies and drift it in lacy jags.

I bequeath myself to the dirt to grow from the grass I love,
If you want me again look for me under your bootsoles.

You will hardly know who I am or what I mean,
But I shall be good health to you nevertheless,
And filter and fibre your blood.

Failing to fetch me at first keep encouraged,
Missing me one place search another,
I stop some where waiting for you

# China Wilds

## *Ezra Pound*

*(1885–1972)*

E ZRA POUND REINVENTED LANGUAGE IN A WAY QUITE
different from Whitman. Rather than making it more or-
ganic and embodied and spontaneous, he attempted to clarify and distill
language, to make it more precise and immediate. In reaction to a po-
etic tradition that had come to be characterized by a highly subjective
language of sentiment, abstraction, decorative metaphor, and rhetorical
embellishment, Pound and a few fellow "imagists" formulated a new idea
of poetry based on the concrete image, and in doing this they were very
self-consciously adapting the strategies of Japanese haiku.

Around the eighth century C.E., Japan sent intellectual emissaries to
China with the mission of mastering Chinese culture and bringing it back
to Japan. All aspects of Chinese culture were then adopted as Japan's own:
philosophy, painting, calligraphy, poetry, even the classical Chinese language
itself. Haiku was one product of this cultural transmission, for it is a distilled
version of the shortest poetic form in ancient China: the briefest Chinese
quatrain form has four lines with five words per line (twenty total), while
haiku has three lines and seventeen word/syllables. And like the Chinese
quatrain, haiku is intensely imagistic and embodies the entire Taoist/Ch'an
conceptual framework (see pp. 7–11) in a particularly concise form.

Haiku was very much in the air and central to the imagists' poetic think-
ing. They often, in fact, wrote haiku. And this influence led them to their

imagist poetic revolution, led by Pound who concisely defined the image in 1913 as "that which presents an intellectual and emotional complex in an instant of time." He further described this new kind of poetry as: direct and imagistic; spare, using the least possible words; and musical in rhythm, rather than following the artificial constraints of rhyme and meter. All of which, of course, describes haiku perfectly. If language is the medium of thought, then the closer language is to things, the closer thought is. Illustrating these ideas, Pound published that same year the most famous poem in the strict imagist model:

IN A STATION OF THE METRO

The apparition of these faces in the crowd;
Petals on a wet, black bough.

In spite of its brevity, this poem may be the most influential poem of the twentieth century, and Pound later described it as a direct extension of classical Japanese haiku:

Three years ago in Paris I got out of a "metro" train at La Concorde, and saw suddenly a beautiful face, and then another and another, and then a beautiful child's face, and then another beautiful woman, and I tried all that day to find words for what this had meant to me, and I could not find any words that seemed to me worthy, or as lovely as that sudden emotion.

. . . A Chinaman said long ago that if a man can't say what he has to say in twelve lines he had better keep quiet. The Japanese have evolved the still shorter form of the *hokku* [i.e., haiku].

"The fallen blossom flies back to its branch:
A butterfly."

. . . The "one image poem" is a form of super-position, that is to say, it is one idea set on top of another. I found it useful in getting out of the impasse in which I had been left by my metro emotion. I wrote a thirty-line poem, and destroyed it because it was what we call work "of second intensity." Six months later I made a poem half that length; a year later I made the following *hokku*-like sentence:—

"The apparition of these faces in the crowd:
Petals, on a wet, black bough."

I dare say it is meaningless unless one has drifted into a certain vein of thought. In a poem of this sort one is trying to record the precise instant when a thing outward and objective transforms itself, or darts into a thing inward and subjective.

With his Metro poem and the poetics surrounding it, Pound unwittingly brought into English poetry the entire Taoist/Ch'an complex of insight (see pp. 7–11). Ch'an too was imported to Japan, where it was known according to the Japanese pronunciation of the word: Zen. And haiku is most essentially an expression of Zen/Ch'an awakening. In that awakening of empty mind, the act of perception becomes a spiritual practice in which the opening of consciousness is a mirror allowing no distinction between inside and outside. Indeed, Pound intuited as much in this description of his "hokku-like" poem as "trying to record the precise instant when a thing outward and objective transforms itself, or darts into a thing inward and subjective." And so, through ancient Chinese thought via haiku, Pound's project effectively replaced the spiritualized subjectivity of the West with an intellectual/emotional world made up of the things around us, thereby opening a deeper form of experience: rather than alienated abstract thought, a language of concrete images allows us to think in concrete things, and therefore to dwell in a more immediate relation to the world. To dwell so deeply, in fact, that consciousness is woven into landscape and Cosmos. Hence, Pound's poetry of images was a poetry of Ch'an enlightenment.

Soon after writing his poem, Pound described the struggle to render his Metro experience slightly differently:

. . . only the other night, wondering how I should tell the adventure, it struck me that in Japan where a work of art is not estimated by its acreage and where sixteen syllables [sic] are counted enough for a poem if you arrange and punctuate them properly, one might make a very little poem which would be translated about as follows: — The apparition of these faces in the crowd; / Petals on a wet, black bough — And there, or in some other very old, very quiet civilisations, some one else might understand the significance.

It is noteworthy here that Pound considered his poem so Japanese that he conceived it as a translation of a poem written in ancient Japan, and he thought it only understandable to someone from ancient Japan or "some other very old, very quiet civilization."

He would soon find that "other very old, very quiet civilization" in China, source of haiku, Zen, and all ancient Japanese culture. Pound's haiku-inspired Imagism was only the beginning of a much larger conceptual revolution. He stumbled into the full picture a year later. Hearing of Pound the imagist through Pound's friend Yone Noguchi, who had written an essay on haiku that was apparently the immediate catalyst for Pound's haiku-like poem, Mary Fenollosa approached him with the unpublished notes and manuscripts of her deceased father, the orientalist Ernest Fenollosa. In Fenollosa's writings on Chinese language and poetry, Pound discovered how Chinese poems are constructed from pictographic ideograms juxtaposed to create constellations of meaning in a poetic field with almost no grammatical structure. This was the very form of poetic thought Pound had been trying to imagine. Using Fenollosa's notes, he translated a group of seventeen Chinese poems (pp. 33–34), in which he created a direct and concrete poetic language in English. He came to think of this poetic form as an "ideogrammic method," an expansion of Imagism in which poetic thought takes on a new complexity as a constellation of image-facts, "luminous details" presented in a direct voice.

Pound's vision gained more explicitly philosophical dimensions when he edited and revised some of Fenollosa's lecture notes, publishing them in 1919 as *The Chinese Written Character as a Medium for Poetry* (p. 35), which has come to be seen almost as much Pound's writing as Fenollosa's because it so perfectly explores and enlarges Pound's imagist thought. The essay, only forty-five small pages in length, is a rambling polemic not without misunderstanding and misguided exaggeration in the details, as critics have been quick to point out. However, it is generally forgotten that Fenollosa lived for many years in Japan, where he moved in the highest cultural circles, and his education in Chinese language and poetry came from classically-trained Japanese scholars (and later, a European-trained scholar at Columbia University). Those Japanese scholars were educated in the classical tradition handed down from China, so Fenollosa's ideas are at least based on a native Chinese/Japanese understanding that should not be easily dismissed.

Building on what he learned in Japan, Fenollosa presents in his essay a group of profound and seminal ideas that make it the most influential American poetic manifesto of the century, providing the theoretical framework that helped make Pound's imagist/ideogrammic poetics the foundation for virtually all poetry afterward. However much individual poets may have adapted or transformed or even reacted against it, even conventional poems are inevitably constructed as a fabric of directly observed image and action, presented in a direct natural language. And Pound intends his poetics to have a revolutionary and broadly philosophical import, his Fenollosa speaking of "the enormous interest of the Chinese language in throwing light upon our forgotten mental processes." And indeed, half a century later, Jacques Derrida claimed that the Fenollosa essay marked an end to Western metaphysics.

The guiding interest of Fenollosa's essay is a poetry that brings language and thought close to things themselves, thereby returning us to a more primal and profound form of experience, to that *contact* Thoreau describes, where we might discover *who* and *where we are*. And rather than Thoreau's terror, *contact* is here an occasion for enlightenment, as it was for Whitman and the ancient Chinese. Here, Fenollosa is describing the experience of belonging to Tao or *tzu-jan* (pp. 7–8): he doesn't use these terms, but as we will see, the concepts are embedded in the ideas he borrows from ancient China.

In essence, the essay proposes a rewilding of self-identity. Remarkably, Fenollosa's discussion assumes throughout that the mind is an integral part of the Cosmos—an assumption acquired from the ancient Chinese conceptual world, both through his Chinese studies and through his immersion in Japanese culture that is based on ancient Chinese culture. He describes the mind as an entity conjured by primitive humans through a system of metaphoric transference wherein language and thought/emotion are created as metaphors based on physical facts in the world. He calls these primal shapers of thought and language "poets," the original and perhaps purest poets, and describes them as hewing to a "scientific" fidelity to empirical facts. The essay contrasts this with the solipsistic "tyranny of logic," which might also be described as the machinery of the Western *soul*, that self-enclosed system of rationalist thought, which the imagist Pound found crystallized in the reigning poetry of subjectivist rhetoric and abstraction and embellishment.

The implications are revelatory. We have lost that primitive sense of connection to things around us, of being part of the movements of natural process, because our thought (language) has drifted far from its sources in the things around us. Renouncing its pictographic roots, it became alphabetic (phonetic), and so words lost their immediate pictographic connections to things. And compounding this, language evolved complex systems of grammar that packaged reality in an intricate mental framework. With its pictographic words and virtually no grammar, classical Chinese avoids these problems, and so became for Pound a model for poetry.

For Fenollosa/Pound, poetry is capable of returning us to a lost experience of dwelling, to thought and expression at that level of primitive immediacy; and this valuation of the primitive as a more authentic and profound form of experience was prescient, for it too becomes a central impulse in the innovative tradition that follows. Pound took the Chinese written language as his exemplar because it still operated at that primitive level of immediacy. In its pictographic ideograms, we witness things themselves in all their concrete immediacy; and so the language represents a system of thought made from the things of this world, as it was for those primitive poets who invented our mental realm. The metaphoric roots of thought/emotion remain visible in the pictographic ideograms of classical Chinese, and its minimalist grammar largely avoids the intricate structures that package the world in a distancing human construction that leaves the mind turning in its own world, "juggling mental counters."

Fenollosa's essay further recognizes that Chinese embodies a more primitive and accurate experience of the world because it does not bifurcate things into dead nouns and living verbs. A Chinese word can generally operate as any part of speech, and so the language recognizes the world as an interrelated system of living processes. This more primitive and accurate perception reflects Taoist philosophical insight (p. 7 ff.) that sees the world as primarily verbal, as flows of Cosmic energy. We tend to see things as noun, and so the world as static, a reflection of our intellectual heritage that values the permanence of abstract idea and spirit. But things we refer to with nouns are in fact verbal processes, moments of transition in that flow of energy; and a poetry of clear images and active verbs could embody and describe that energy flow.

Although English poetry can never equal Chinese for primal immediacy, Pound thought it should aspire to approach that immediacy. And here we have returned to Pound's original imagist poetics: a language spare and concrete and active (verbal), with no unnecessary grammatical or rhetorical complications, and relying for thought and expression on images, on things themselves. In this, poetry can return us to a more embodied and primitive awareness, which is nothing other than Thoreau's *contact*.

It is an interesting study in inter-cultural translation. Language, Taoist/Ch'an thought and practice, the arts: all dimensions of ancient Chinese culture are interrelated, manifestations of a single conceptual framework; so when Pound brings a few of these dimensions into Western culture, he implicitly brings all the others. When he talks about pictographic language and imagist poetics, he is also talking about a Ch'an mirroring of the particulars in that dynamic Cosmos (*tzu-jan*). With that mirroring comes thinking in things and the spiritual practice of empty mind, both of which weave consciousness wholly into the generative movements of the Cosmos. When he talks in his Imagist principles about a poetry following musical rhythm rather than artificial constraints of rhyme and meter, he is also talking about practicing *wu-wei* (see p. 8), acting as part of *tzu-jan*'s perennial unfurling. Fenollosa says nothing specific about the Chinese philosophical world—but when he proposes that reality is verbal, always in motion, he is essentially proposing the Taoist Cosmos as a living organism, female and generative and in perpetual transformation. Indeed, he speaks of "lines of force [that] pulse through things," which is a concise definiton of *ch'i*, the breath-force that animates all things in the living Taoist Cosmos. At bottom, this all but unspoken philosophical framework is the conceptual revolution that Pound handed down to the tradition that followed.

Pound's interests eventually moved elsewhere. Rather than creating a body of imagist/ideogrammic poetry, he followed the grand aspirations of his *Cantos*, an eight-hundred-page epic poem, in which ideogrammic structure becomes a sweeping patchwork of erudition. But at the end of his life, in the *Cantos*'s poignant final poem, he harkens back to the simplicity and directness of his imagist roots:

I have tried to write Paradise

Do not move
    Let the wind speak
        that is paradise.

Let the Gods forgive what I
        have made
Let those I love try to forgive
        what I have made.

The task of putting Pound's imagist/ideogrammic insights into practice fell to his poetic descendants, chief among them being the poets presented in this book. In fact, poetic expression by means of immediate and concrete images, that poetics of Ch'an enlightenment, became the operating assumption that shaped virtually all of twentieth-century poetry in America. And the same is true of his "musical rhythm" which became, as we will see, breath-driven organic form. A revolution indeed.

# THE RIVER-MERCHANT'S WIFE: A LETTER

While my hair was still cut straight across my forehead
I played about the front gate, pulling flowers.
You came by on bamboo stilts, playing horse,
You walked about my seat, playing with blue plums.
And we went on living in the village of Chōkan:
Two small people, without dislike or suspicion.

At fourteen I married My Lord you.
I never laughed, being bashful.
Lowering my head, I looked at the wall.
Called to, a thousand times, I never looked back.

At fifteen I stopped scowling,
I desired my dust to be mingled with yours
Forever and forever and forever.
Why should I climb the look out?

At sixteen you departed,
You sent into far Ku-tō-en, by the river of swirling eddies,
And you have been gone five months.
The monkeys make sorrowful noise overhead.

You dragged your feet when you went out.
By the gate now, the moss is grown, the different mosses,
Too deep to clear them away!
The leaves fall early this autumn, in wind.
The paired butterflies are already yellow with August
over the grass in the West garden;
They hurt me. I grow older.
If you are coming down through the narrows of the river Kiang,
Please let me know beforehand,
And I will come out to meet you
        As far as Chō-fū-Sa.

                  *Li Po*

# THE JEWEL STAIRS' GRIEVANCE

The jewelled steps are already quite white with dew,
It is so late that the dew soaks my gauze stockings,
And I let down the crystal curtain
And watch the moon through the clear autumn.

*Li Po*

# SEPARATION ON THE RIVER KIANG

Ko-jin goes west from Kō-kaku-ro,
The smoke-flowers are blurred over the river.
His lone sail blots the far sky.
And now I see only the river,
      The long Kiang, reaching heaven.

*Li Po*

## *from* THE CHINESE WRITTEN CHARACTER AS A MEDIUM FOR POETRY

Thought is successive, not through some accident or weakness of our subjective operations but because the operations of nature are successive.

———

Chinese notation is something much more than arbitrary symbols. It is based upon a vivid shorthand picture of the operations of nature.

———

In reading Chinese we do not seem to be juggling mental counters, but to be watching *things* work out their own fate.

———

A true noun, an isolated thing, does not exist in nature. Things are only the terminal points, or rather the meeting points, of actions, cross-sections cut through actions, snapshots. Neither can a pure verb, an abstract motion, be possible in nature. The eye sees noun and verb as one: things in motion, motion in things, and so the Chinese conception tends to represent them.

———

. . . the discredited, or rather the useless, logic of the Middle Ages. According to this logic, thought deals with abstractions, concepts drawn out of things by a sifting process. These logicians never inquired how the "qualities" which they pulled out of things came to be there. The truth of all their little checker-board juggling depended upon the natural order by which these powers or properties or qualities were folded in concrete things, yet they despised the "thing" as a mere "particular," or pawn. It was as if Botany should reason from the leaf-patterns woven into our table-cloths. Valid scientific thought consists in following as closely as may be the actual and entangled lines of forces as they pulse through things. Thought deals with no bloodless concepts but watches *things move* under its microscope.

The sentence form was forced upon primitive men by nature itself. It was not we who made it; it was a reflection of the temporal order in causation. All truth has to be expressed in sentences because all truth is the *transference of power. . . .*

This brings language close to *things*.

. . . how poetical is the Chinese form and how close to nature. In translating Chinese, verse especially, we must hold as closely as possible to the concrete force of the original.

Like nature, the Chinese words are alive and plastic, because *thing* and *action* are not formally separated. The Chinese language naturally knows no grammar.

The fact is that almost every written Chinese word is . . . *not* abstract. It is not exclusive of parts of speech, but comprehensive; not something which is neither a noun, verb, nor adjective, but something which is all of them at once.

. . . the enormous interest of the Chinese language in throwing light upon our forgotten mental processes . . .

Chinese poetry demands that we abandon our narrow grammatical categories.

You will ask, how could the Chinese have built up a great intellectual fabric from mere picture writing? To the ordinary Western mind, which believes that thought is concerned with logical categories and which rather condemns the faculty of direct imagination, this feat seems quite impossible. Yet the Chinese language with its peculiar materials has passed over from the seen to the unseen by exactly the same process which all ancient races employed. This process is metaphor, the use of material images to suggest immaterial relations.

The whole delicate substance of speech is built upon substrata of metaphor. Abstract terms, pressed by etymology, reveal their ancient roots still embedded in direct action. But the primitive metaphors do not spring from arbitrary *subjective* processes. They are possible only because they follow objective lines of relations in nature herself.

It is a mistake to suppose, with some philosophers of aesthetics, that art and poetry aim to deal with the general and the abstract. This misconception has been foisted upon us by mediaeval logic. Art and poetry deal with the concrete of nature. . . . Metaphor, its chief device, is at once the substance of nature and of language. Poetry only does consciously what the primitive races did unconsciously. The chief work of literary men . . . lies in feeling back along the ancient lines of advance.

---

I believe that the Chinese written language has not only absorbed the poetic substance of nature and built with it a second work of metaphor, but has, through its very pictorial visibility, been able to retain its original creative poetry with far more vigor and vividness than any phonetic tongue.

Our ancestors built the accumulations of metaphor into structures of language and into systems of thought.

---

There is little or nothing in a phonetic word to exhibit the embryonic stages of its growth. It does not bear its metaphor on its face. . . .

In this, Chinese shows its advantage. Its etymology is constantly visible. It retains the creative impulse and process, visible and at work. After thousands of years the lines of metaphoric advance are still shown. . . . The very soil of Chinese life seems entangled in the roots of its [language].

---

The true formula for thought is: The cherry tree is all that it does. Its correlated verbs compose it. At bottom these verbs are transitive. Such verbs may be almost infinite in number.

In diction and in grammatical form science is utterly opposed to logic. Primitive men who created language agreed with science and not with logic. Logic has abused the language which they left to her mercy.

Poetry agrees with science and not with logic.

The moment we use the copula, the moment we express subjective inclusions, poetry evaporates. The more concretely and vividly we express the interactions of things the better the poetry. We need in poetry thousands of active words, each doing its utmost to show forth the motive and vital forces. We can not exhibit the wealth of nature by mere summation, by the piling of sentences. Poetic thought works by suggestion, crowding maximum meaning into the single phrase pregnant, charged, and luminous from within.

In Chinese, each word accumulated this sort of energy in itself.

Should we pass formally to the study of Chinese poetry, we should warn ourselves against logicianised pitfalls. . . . We should be ware of English grammar, its hard parts of speech, and its lazy satisfaction with nouns and adjectives. We should seek and at least bear in mind the verbal undertone of each noun. We should avoid "is" and bring in a wealth of neglected English verbs.

––––––––––

Chinese poetry gets back near to the processes of nature by means of its vivid [image], its wealth of such [image].

––––––––––

The prehistoric poets who created language discovered the whole harmonious framework of nature.

# Local Wilds

## *William Carlos Williams*

## *(1883–1963)*

P OUND'S IDEAS WERE ADOPTED AND TRANSFORMED IN a range of singular and surprising ways across the tradition of innovative poets to come later in the twentieth century, first among them William Carlos Williams, with whom Pound shared an enduring literary friendship that began when they met in college. Williams spent his entire adult life in the same modest town—Rutherford, New Jersey—which was semi-rural well into his middle age. His schooling was cosmopolitan, in Switzerland and at the University of Pennsylvania, but he chose to return to his hometown where he practiced medicine and pursued a poetic commitment to local and everyday experience. This commitment amounts to a kind of anti-poetry, in fact, because he made poetry from the most ordinary and seemingly unpoetic material, infusing it with genuine affection, childlike wonder, and a warm sense of humor.

For Williams the doctor, poetry represented a remedy to a problem he diagnosed in the introduction to his breakthrough book, *Spring and All* (1923): "There is a constant barrier between the reader and his consciousness of immediate contact with the world." *Contact*, Thoreau's word again, and Williams continues much in the vein of Thoreau's query on Mount Ktaadn:

> the thing [a person] never knows and never dares to know is what he is at the exact moment that he is. And this moment is the only thing in which I am at all interested.

So Williams's poetry becomes a response to Thoreau's impossible question, a way to return us to that experience of *contact*. And as with Whitman and Pound, this *contact* is not at all an occasion for terror. Quite the contrary, Williams saw it as self-revelation.

In addition to the direct influence of Pound's Imagism, Williams too was influenced by the then widely popular haiku form. He wrote numerous haiku in the years prior to his first publications, and the quintessential Williams poem can be seen as an extended haiku, or perhaps a series of linked haiku-like stanzas. Williams's innovations became central to the avant-garde tradition that followed, generating wildly diverse poetic practices. His poetry seems clear, direct, simple, and plainspoken: an "artless Imagism," but that concept contains considerable philosophical complexity, philosophical complexity that clearly reflects the ancient Taoist/ Ch'an ideas carried below the surface in haiku, Pound's imagist poetics and Chinese translations, and the Fenollosa essay.

Unlike Pound, for whom the image is a carefully chosen moment that "presents an intellectual and emotional complex in an instant of time," Williams avoids poeticizing the real. He prefers to leave things as they are in all their ordinariness. This represents a step beyond Pound in terms of rewilding consciousness, for it brought mind as close as possible to Ch'an's "immediate contact with the world," to the routine flow of actual experience, the actual texture of day-to-day life: *tzu-jan*, things in and of themselves. Williams famously summarized this in an almost too perfect and too quotable axiom that insistently recurs in his writing, notably numerous times in his epic poem *Paterson*, based on the city as "an image large enough to embody the whole knowable world about me":

> For the poet there are no ideas but in things.
>
> . . . no ideas but in things.
>
> —Say it, no ideas but in things—
>
> —No ideas but in the facts . . .
>
> Not prophecy! NOT prophecy!
>            but the thing itself!

This insistence reminds us that we can trace *idea* back to the Greek *idein* and the Indo-European root *weid*, both meaning "to see" in the direct physical sense of seeing an object in the world: so, not an abstract concept, but the physical content of sight.

Williams's poems are meant to have an emotional impact, to make us *feel* things themselves, or perhaps even to let things feel themselves in us (though he would not have quite said it this way). Williams wants to reveal the emotional content inherent to things in and of themselves, not imposed by humanity:

> Writing is not a searching about in the daily experience for apt similes and pretty thoughts and images, [for that] destroys, makes nature an accessory to the particular theory he is following, it blinds him to his world.

That is, the poems with their tenderness and love cultivate an *attentiveness* to things, and that is the basis for *contact*, for the reweaving of consciousness and Cosmos.

For Williams, the mind's efforts to shape and understand experience are also a part of natural process, as much so as a river flowing or flower blooming:

> poetry . . . affirms reality most powerfully and therefore . . . creates a new object, a play, a dance which is not a mirror up to nature but—

This leads to a poetry remarkably at ease, responding spontaneously and effortlessly to everyday experience, a poetry of *wu-wei*: artless and improvisational (prefiguration of Olson's poetics), as opposed to the traditional poetic practice of the Western rationalist and otherworldly "soul," a practice that involved careful choice of appropriate subject matter and intricate crafting of an artificially dense and formalized language. At the same time, the poem is itself an "object," a thing in the world. It is an act of nature made by a primate body, its words having an ontological status no different than a stand of poplar trees or a herd of elk.

Though Williams wrote poems in a broad range of size and shape, the result of a sensibility responding freely and spontaneously to the range of experience, his poetic thought appears most clearly in his signature poems: brief, and with very short lines. The short chiseled lines and their off-kilter line breaks were all but unprecedented in English poetry. Indeed, they were a revolution, the first time poetry was organized primarily as a *visual* event on the page. Here is another extension of Pound's discovery in

Chinese of a visual language. It was a new poetic form meant to emphasize "things" themselves (*tzu-jan*), the "ideas" of the poem. It forces a reader to slow down and *attend* to things: not necessarily rare or captivating things, compelling or dramatic things, but routine and unexceptional things, as in the iconic wheelbarrow poem:

## THE RED WHEELBARROW

so much depends
upon

a red wheel
barrow

glazed with rain
water

beside the white
chickens

Here, the line breaks force us to weigh *wheel* and *barrow* as separate entities before combining them into *wheel barrow*, *rain* and *water* before *rain water*, *white* and *chickens* before *white chickens*.

At the same time, Williams's new poetic form emphasizes the physicality of the language itself, forcing readers to encounter the presence of words and their relationships, and the quiet music of the poem as a "thing," as "a new object, a play, a dance which is not a mirror up to nature but—." Just as Williams values all experience equally, even the most everyday, he values words equally, using short lines with their frequent breaks to emphasize the little everyday words we tend not to notice or value particularly: articles, prepositions, conjunctions. And if words are the material of thought, this is to value any piece of thought equally. So even while Williams's poetry cultivates an attention to the facts of the world itself (*tzu-jan*), it also cultivates an attention to the facts of the mind itself, the mind too as *tzu-jan*. And miraculously, in a poem of "no ideas but in things," the two become one and the same: objective and subjective a single living tissue. It is Williams's way of rewilding consciousness, of dwelling as integral to *tzu-jan*'s ongoing transformations.

# THE LOCUST TREE IN FLOWER

Among
of
green

stiff
old
bright

broken
branch
come

white
sweet
May

again

# THE LOCUST TREE IN FLOWER

Among
the leaves
bright

green
of wrist-thick
tree

and old
stiff broken
branch

ferncool
swaying
loosely strung—

come May
again
white blossom

clusters
hide
to spill

their sweets
almost
unnoticed

down
and quickly
fall

## TO A POOR OLD WOMAN

munching a plum on
the street a paper bag
of them in her hand

They taste good to her
They taste good
to her. They taste
good to her

You can see it by
the way she gives herself
to the one half
sucked out in her hand

Comforted
a solace of ripe plums
seeming to fill the air
They taste good to her

# SUMMER SONG

Wanderer moon
smiling a
faintly ironical smile
at this
brilliant, dew-moistened
summer morning,—
a detached
sleepily indifferent
smile, a
wanderer's smile,—
if I should
buy a shirt
your color and
put on a necktie
sky-blue
where would they carry me?

## THE RIGHT OF WAY

In passing with my mind
on nothing in the world

but the right of way
I enjoy on the road by

virtue of the law—
I saw

an elderly man who
smiled and looked away

to the north past a house—
a woman in blue

who was laughing and
leaning forward to look up

into the man's half
averted face

and a boy of eight who was
looking at the middle of

the man's belly
at a watchchain—

The supreme importance
of this nameless spectacle

sped me by them
without a word—

Why bother where I went?
for I went spinning on the

four wheels of my car
along the wet road until

I saw a girl with one leg
over the rail of a balcony


## THE WILDFLOWER

Black eyed susan
rich orange
round the purple core

the white daisy
is not enough

Crowds are white
as farmers
who live poorly

But you
are rich
in savagery—

Arab
Indian
dark woman.

## POEM

As the cat
climbed over
the top of

the jamcloset
first the right
forefoot

carefully
then the hind
stepped down

into the pit of
the empty
flowerpot

# BETWEEN WALLS

the black wings
of the

hospital where
nothing

will grow lie
cinders

in which shine
the broken

pieces of a green
bottle

# FINE WORK WITH PITCH AND COPPER

Now they are resting
in the fleckless light
separately in unison

like the sacks
of sifted stone stacked
regularly by twos

about the flat roof
ready after lunch
to be opened and strewn

The copper in eight
foot strips has been
beaten lengthwise

down the center at right
angles and lies ready
to edge the coping

One still chewing
picks up a copper strip
and runs his eye along it

# YOUNG WOMAN AT A WINDOW

She sits with
tears on

her cheek
her cheek on

her hand
the child

in her lap
his nose

pressed
to the glass

# AUTUMN

A stand of people
by an open

grave underneath
the heavy leaves

celebrates
the cut and fill

for the new road
where

an old man
on his knees

reaps a basket-
ful of

matted grasses for
his goats

# PICTURE OF A NUDE IN A MACHINE SHOP

and foundry,
    (that's art)
    a red ostrich plume
in her hair:

Sweat and muddy water,
coiled fuse-strips
    surround her
poised sitting—
(between red, parted
    curtains)

the right leg
    (stockinged)
up!
    beside the point—
at ease.

Light as a glove, light
as her black gloves!
Modeled as a shoe, a woman's
high heeled shoe!

—the other leg stretched
out
    bare
    (toward the top—
and upward)
        as
the smeared hide under
shirt and pants
stiff with grease and dirt
is bare—
    approaching
the centrum

(disguised)
the metal to be devalued!

   —bare as
a blow-torch flame,
     undisguised.


## BREAKFAST

Twenty sparrows
on

a scattered
turd:

Share and share
alike.

# SUZANNE

Brother Paul! look!
—but he rushes to a different
window.
The moon!

I heard shrieks and thought:
What's that?

That's just Suzanne
talking to the moon!
Pounding on the window
with both fists:

    Paul!       Paul!

—and talking to the moon.
Shrieking
and pounding the glass
with both fists!

Brother Paul! the moon!

# Coastal Wilds

## *Robinson Jeffers*
### *(1887–1962)*

W HILE POUND AND WILLIAMS RESHAPED LANGUAGE
to reestablish "immediate contact with the world," with
the actual material of our lives, they were working from within a human-
centered perspective. Jeffers operates outside of that perspective. He speaks
with the elemental voice of the planet itself, the "solid earth" and "actual
world" Thoreau *contacts* in that moment when he sees himself and reality
clean. This voice is most clear in Jeffers's short lyric poems, such as the
archetypal "Continent's End" (p. 62), where Jeffers takes on the same ele-
mental status as the sea he addresses as "mother." Often using commas
rather than periods between sentences to create momentum rising through
the poem, he uses long booming lines that move with the cadences of the
sea pounding against the continent's edge, and indeed the cadences of
some deeper source that he shares with the sea.

> Mother, though my song's measure is like your surf-beat's ancient
> rhythm I never learned it of you.
> Before there was any water there were tides of fire, both our tones
> flow from the older fountain.

Remarkably, however elemental this voice is, it is the voice of Jeffers's
everyday immediate experience. With his wife, Jeffers moved at the age of

twenty-seven to Carmel-by-the-Sea, then a small village on the Northern California coast. He apprenticed himself to a stonemason, and thereby built a house of stone looking out over the sea on a relatively pristine stretch of granite coastline a few miles south of the village. Just as Williams made a poetry of his locale, Jeffers made a poetry of his: the wild California coast. The raw seascape and his physical work with stone came together in a kind of magical alchemy for Jeffers, a gradual enlightenment experience that led to a singular poetic vision, a vision first voiced in *Tamar and Other Poems*, published in 1924, the year after Williams's *Spring and All*. Jeffers lived far from Europe and the East Coast, and his work was far outside the mainstream of literary Modernism. He had little interest in formal experimentation; he was pursuing an explicitly philosophical vision:

> I believe that the universe is one being, all its parts are different expressions of the same energy, and they are all in communication with each other, influencing each other, therefore parts of one organic whole. (This is physics, I believe, as well as religion.) The parts change and pass, or die, people and races and rocks and stars, none of them seems to me important in itself, but only the whole. This whole is in all its parts so beautiful, and is felt by me to be so intensely in earnest, that I am compelled to love it, and to think of it as divine. It seems to me that this whole alone is worthy of the deeper sort of love; and that here is peace, freedom, I might say a kind of salvation, in turning one's affection outward toward this one God, rather than inward on one's self, or on humanity, or on human imagination and abstractions. . . .

Here we see again that interest in direct *contact* with "The solid earth! The actual world!" Jeffers's impulse was to probe the philosophical implications of this experience of *contact*. In this, he was caught at the terminological limit of Christianity and nineteenth-century Romanticism, still depending on divinity to explain his experience of a Cosmos so wondrous. In this, Jeffers represents an extension of the pantheist line from Deists and Romantics through Thoreau and Whitman, but with two additions: (1) Jeffers is wholly a part of the divine wild, while his predecessors generally saw themselves as separate and looking out on divine wilderness; (2) that wilderness is utterly indifferent to human concerns, elemental and indifferent as the vast stone basement beneath the continent.

Sometimes Jeffers uses the cooler "it," which was truer to the reality of his vision. But he uses the term *God* in numerous poems, perhaps most notably in the phrase: *the wild God of the world*. That it is a terminological placeholder, a kind of cultural image evoking breathtaking splendor, is suggested by his use of the wild swan, the thundering storm of its huge wings, when virtually the same phrase appears in another poem (p. 66): "this wild swan of a world."

Poets often write more than they know. If Jeffers had encountered ancient Chinese thought, he might have called the universe Tao, for he shares with Lao Tzu a vision of reality as a single living "organic whole" whose most fundamental nature is change and transformation. And he shares the assumption (now translated into American poetry via Fenollosa/Pound) that it is through "immediate contact with the world" that one dwells as integral to that "organic whole." Lao Tzu describes his Tao in lines that also struggle with terminology, but might almost be a gloss on "Continent's End," with its "mother" and "older fountain":

> There was something all murky shadow,
> born before heaven and earth:
>
> o such utter silence, utter emptiness.
>
> Isolate and changeless,
> it moves everywhere without fail:
>
> picture the mother of all beneath heaven.
>
> I don't know its name.
> I'll call it *Tao*,
> and if I must name it, name it *Vast*.

Jeffers inhabits time at vast scales of elemental transformation, scales at which linear time is replaced by a unity of time and space moving like Lao Tzu's ongoing generative moment (p. 8). And Jeffers shares with Lao Tzu and China's classical poets the recognition that even as we humans belong to it as integral parts, this organic Cosmos has no particular interest in our welfare.

If Jeffers's thought appears heartlessly misanthropic in its indifference to human welfare, it is simply a reflection of how deeply he identifies with the elemental Cosmos. And if that misanthropy sometimes seems overbearing and polemical, it is because he is struggling against the entire Western tradition, in which the human is assumed to be qualitatively separate from and superior to everything else in the material universe. Jeffers blames this assumption for virtually all evil—especially war and environmental destruction. He believes humans have become too numerous, too self-involved and self-important in their greed, too ruthless and destructive. It is a belief that would become commonplace in intellectual circles and for many poets to come in this ecopoetic tradition. Jeffers assumes humans are, in their basic natures, animal and good; but that the assumptions of Western civilization have cut humans off from their true selves as part of the larger whole, and that their success as a species had become a blight on that whole. Like many poets in this book, he thought we need to return to a more primitive level of existence and consciousness:

> We must uncenter our minds from ourselves;
> We must unhumanize our views a little, and become confident
> As the rock and ocean that we were made from.

For Jeffers, we humans are our beautiful and true and elemental selves only when we are in *contact*, for only then do we wholly belong to the larger whole. This belief that we should return to primal levels of identity and culture is no different from Lao Tzu's vision of sage wisdom as belonging to the ontological process of Tao. It is the essence of deep ecology as a radical critique of the separation between consciousness and earth, and why Jeffers marks the manifest beginning of a modern American ecopoetric tradition. And it is Jeffers's answer to Thoreau's questions: *Who are we? Where are we?* In fact, Jeffers reveals the Western assumptions lurking in Thoreau's first question, assumptions that predetermine any possible answer. The question should be: "What are we," for the "who" assumes some kind of self or spirit-center separate from the "where." But in Jeffers *who we are* is integral to *where we are*:

A severed hand
Is an ugly thing, and man* dissevered from the earth and stars and
    his history . . . for contemplation or in fact . . .
Often appears atrociously ugly. Integrity is wholeness, the greatest
    beauty is
Organic wholeness, the wholeness of life and things, the divine
    beauty of the universe. Love that, not man
Apart from that. . . .

---

* It is impossible not to cringe at such usages, here and in many of these male poets
who worked before sexist language conventions were challenged.

# CONTINENT'S END

At the equinox when the earth was veiled in a late rain, wreathed with
    wet poppies, waiting spring,
The ocean swelled for a far storm and beat its boundary, the ground-swell
    shook the beds of granite.

I gazing at the boundaries of granite and spray, the established sea-marks,
    felt behind me
Mountain and plain, the immense breadth of the continent, before me
    the mass and doubled stretch of water.

I said: You yoke the Aleutian seal-rocks with the lava and coral sowings
    that flower the south,
Over your flood the life that sought the sunrise faces ours that has
    followed the evening star.

The long migrations meet across you and it is nothing to you, you have
    forgotten us, mother.
You were much younger when we crawled out of the womb and lay in
    the sun's eye on the tideline.

It was long and long ago; we have grown proud since then and you have
    grown bitter; life retains
Your mobile soft unquiet strength; and envies hardness, the insolent
    quietness of stone.

The tides are in our veins, we still mirror the stars, life is your child, but
    there is in me
Older and harder than life and more impartial, the eye that watched
    before there was an ocean.

That watched you fill your beds out of the condensation of thin vapor and
    watched you change them,
That saw you soft and violent wear your boundaries down, eat rock, shift
    places with the continents.

Mother, though my song's measure is like your surf-beat's ancient rhythm
    I never learned it of you.
Before there was any water there were tides of fire, both our tones flow
    from the older fountain.


NATURAL MUSIC


The old voice of the ocean, the bird-chatter of little rivers,
(Winter has given them gold for silver
To stain their water and bladed green for brown to line their banks)
From different throats intone one language.
So I believe if we were strong enough to listen without
Divisions of desire and terror
To the storm of the sick nations, the rage of the hunger-smitten cities,
Those voices also would be found
Clean as a child's; or like some girl's breathing who dances alone
By the ocean-shore, dreaming of lovers.

# NOVEMBER SURF

Some lucky day each November great waves awake and are drawn
Like smoking mountains bright from the west
And come and cover the cliff with white violent cleanness: then suddenly
The old granite forgets half a year's filth:
The orange-peel, egg-shells, papers, pieces of clothing, the clots
Of dung in corners of the rock, and used
Sheaths that make light love safe in the evenings: all the droppings of the
     summer
Idlers washed off in a winter ecstasy:
I think this cumbered continent envies its cliff then. . . . But all seasons
The earth, in her childlike prophetic sleep,
Keeps dreaming of the bath of a storm that prepares up the long coast
Of the future to scour more than her sea-lines:
The cities gone down, the people fewer and the hawks more numerous,
The rivers mouth to source pure; when the two-footed
Mammal, being someways one the nobler animals, regains
The dignity of room, the value of rareness.

# ROCK AND HAWK

Here is a symbol in which
Many high tragic thoughts
Watch their own eyes.

This gray rock, standing tall
On the headland, where the sea-wind
Lets no tree grow,

Earthquake-proved, and signatured
By ages of storms: on its peak
A falcon has perched.

I think, here is your emblem
To hand in the future sky;
Not the cross, not the hive,

But this; bright power, dark peace;
Fierce consciousness joined with final
Disinterestedness;

Life with calm death; the falcon's
Realist eyes and act
Married to the massive

Mysticism of stone,
Which failure cannot cast down
Nor success make proud.

# LOVE THE WILD SWAN

"I hate my verses, every line, every word.
Oh pale and brittle pencils ever to try
One grass-blade's curve, or the throat of one bird
That clings to twig, ruffled against white sky.
Oh cracked and twilight mirrors ever to catch
One color, one glinting flash, of the splendor of things.
Unlucky hunter, Oh bullets of wax,
The lion beauty, the wild-swan wings, the storm of the wings."
— This wild swan of a world is no hunter's game.
Better bullets than yours would miss the white breast,
Better mirrors than yours would crack in the flame.
Does it matter whether you hate your . . . self? At least
Love your eyes that can see, your mind that can
Hear the music, the thunder of the wings. Love the wild swan.

# GRAY WEATHER

It is true that, older than man and ages to outlast him, the Pacific surf
Still cheerfully pounds the worn granite drum;
But there's no storm; and the birds are still, no song; no kind of excess;
Nothing that shines, nothing is dark;
There is neither joy nor grief nor a person, the sun's tooth sheathed in cloud,
And life has no more desires than a stone.
The stormy conditions of time and change are all abrogated, the essential
Violences of survival, pleasure,
Love, wrath and pain, and the curious desire of knowing, all perfectly suspended.
In the cloudy light, in the timeless quietness,
One explores deeper than the nerves or heart of nature, the womb or soul,
To the bone, the careless white bone, the excellence.

# HURT HAWKS

## I.

The broken pillar of the wing jags from the clotted shoulder,
The wing trails like a banner in defeat,
No more to use the sky forever but live with famine
And pain a few days: cat nor coyote
Will shorten the week of waiting for death, there is game without talons.
He stands under the oak-bush and waits
The lame feet of salvation; at night he remembers freedom
And flies in a dream, the dawns ruin it.
He is strong and pain is worse to the strong, incapacity is worse.
The curs of the day come and torment him
At distance, no one but death the redeemer will humble that head,
The intrepid readiness, the terrible eyes.
The wild God of the world is sometimes merciful to those
That ask mercy, not often to the arrogant.
You do not know him, you communal people, or you have forgotten him;
Intemperate and savage, the hawk remembers him;
Beautiful and wild, the hawks, and men that are dying, remember him.

## II.

I'd sooner, except the penalties, kill a man than a hawk; but the great redtail
Had nothing left but unable misery
From the bone too shattered for mending, the wing that trailed under his
    talons when he moved.
We had fed him six weeks, I gave him freedom,
He wandered over the foreland hill and returned in the evening, asking
    for death,
Not like a beggar, still eyed with the old
Implacable arrogance. I gave him the lead gift in the twilight. What fell
    was relaxed,
Owl-downy, soft feminine feathers; but what
Soared: the fierce rush: the night-herons by the flooded river cried fear at
    its rising
Before it was quite unsheathed from reality.

# NEW MEXICAN MOUNTAIN

I watch the Indians dancing to help the young corn at Taos pueblo. The
     old men squat in a ring
And make the song, the young women with fat bare arms, and a few
     shame-faced young men, shuffle the dance.

The lean-muscled young men are naked to the narrow loins, their breasts
     and backs daubed with white clay,
Two eagle-feathers plume the black heads. They dance with reluctance,
     they are growing civilized; the old men persuade them.

Only the drum is confident, it thinks the world has not changed; the
     beating heart, the simplest of rhythms,
It thinks the world has not changed at all; it is only a dreamer, a brainless
     heart, the drum has no eyes.

These tourists have eyes, the hundred watching the dance, white
     Americans, hungrily too, with reverence, not laughter;
Pilgrims from civilization, anxiously seeking beauty, religion, poetry;
     pilgrims from the vacuum.

People from cities, anxious to be human again. Poor show how they suck
     you empty! The Indians are emptied,
And certainly there was never religion enough, nor beauty nor poetry
     here . . . to fill Americans.

Only the drum is confident, it thinks the world has not changed.
     Apparently only myself and the strong
Tribal drum, and the rockhead of Taos mountain, remember that
     civilization is a transient sickness.

# THE EYE

The Atlantic is a stormy moat; and the Mediterranean,
The blue pool in the old garden,
More than five thousand years has drunk sacrifice
Of ships and blood, and shines in the sun; but here the Pacific:—
Our ships, planes, wars are perfectly irrelevant.
Neither our present blood-feud with the brave dwarfs
Nor any future world-quarrel of westering
And eastering man, the bloody migrations, greed of power, clash of faiths—
Is a speck of dust on the great scale-pan.
Here from this mountain shore, headland beyond stormy headland
    plunging like dolphins through the blue sea-smoke
Into pale sea,—look west at the hill of water: it is half the planet: this dome,
    this half-globe, this bulging
Eyeball of water, arched over to Asia,
Australia and white Antarctica: those are the eyelids that never close; this is
    the staring unsleeping
Eye of the earth; and what it watches is not our wars.

## OCTOBER WEEK-END

It is autumn still, but at three in the morning
All the magnificent wonders of midwinter midnight, blue dog-star,
Orion, red Aldebaran, the ermine-fur Pleiades,
Parading above the gable of the house. Their music is their shining,
And the house beats like a heart with dance-music
Because our boys have grown to the age when girls are their music.
There is wind in the trees, and the gray ocean's
Music on the rock. I am warming my blood with starlight, not with girls' eyes,
But really the night is quite mad with music.

## CARMEL POINT

The extraordinary patience of things!
This beautiful place defaced with a crop of suburban houses—
How beautiful when we first beheld it,
Unbroken field of poppy and lupin walled with clean cliffs;
No intrusion but two or three horses pasturing,
Or a few milch cows rubbing their flanks on the outcrop rock-heads—
No the spoiler has come: does it care?
Not faintly. It has all time. It knows the people are a tide
That swells and in time will ebb, and all
Their works dissolve. Meanwhile the image of the pristine beauty
Lives in the very grain of the granite,
Safe as the endless ocean that climbs our cliff.—As for us:
We must uncenter our minds from ourselves;
We must unhumanize our views a little, and become confident
As the rock and ocean that we were made from.

# THE DEER LAY DOWN THEIR BONES

I followed the narrow cliffside trail half way up the mountain
Above the deep river-canyon. There was a little cataract crossed the path,
      flinging itself
Over tree roots and rocks, shaking the jewelled fern-fronds, bright bubbling
      water
Pure from the mountain, but a bad smell came up. Wondering at it I
      clambered down the steep stream
Some forty feet, and found in the midst of bush-oak and laurel,
Hung like a bird's nest on the precipice brink a small hidden clearing,
Grass and a shallow pool. But all about there were bones lying in the grass,
      clean bones and stinking bones,
Antlers and bones: I understood that the place was a refuge for wounded
      deer; there are so many
Hurt ones escape the hunters and limp away to lie hidden; here they have
      water for the awful thirst
And peace to die in; dense green laurel and grim cliff
Make sanctuary, and a sweet wind blows upward from the deep gorge. —
      I wish my bones were with theirs.

But that's a foolish thing to confess, and a little cowardly. We know that life
Is on the whole quite equally good and bad, mostly gray neutral, and can
      be endured
To the dim end, no matter what magic of grass, water and precipice, and
      pain of wounds,
Makes death look dear. We have been given life and have used it—not a
      great gift perhaps—but in honesty
Should use it all. Mine's empty since my love died—Empty? The
      flame-haired grandchild with great blue eyes
That look like hers?—What can I do for the child? I gaze at her and wonder
      what sort of man
In the fall of the world . . . I am growing old, that is the trouble. My
      children and little grandchildren
Will find their way, and why should I wait ten years yet, having lived
      sixty-seven, ten years more or less,

Before I crawl out on a ledge of rock and die snapping, like a wolf
Who has lost his mate?—I am bound by my own thirty-year-old decision: who drinks the wine
Should take the dregs; even in the bitter lees and sediment
New discovery may lie. The deer in that beautiful place lay down their bones: I must wear mine.

# Mountain Wilds

## *Kenneth Rexroth*

*(1905–1982)*

J EFFERS MARKS THE BEGINNING OF AN ALTERNATIVE
poetic tradition far removed from the literary centers of the East,
ecopoetic and based in landscape. Kenneth Rexroth is the second major
poet in that tradition, publishing his first mature poems in the forties.
While landscape meant the wild Pacific coast for Jeffers, it meant Califor-
nia's mountains for Rexroth, especially the high peaks of the Sierra Nevada
range. He spent large amounts of time camping in the Sierra, his moun-
tain wanderings often lasting months at a stretch. Rexroth wrote most of
his great poetry there in the breathtaking "range of light," home ground for
John Muir and the American environmental movement; so it makes per-
fect sense that he found his poetic voice through classical Chinese poetry,
a tradition infused with mountains and rivers.

In his mid-teens, Rexroth discovered Pound's translations of Li Po. At
eighteen he visited Taos, New Mexico, itself a landscape of consuming
beauty, where he met the poet-translator Witter Bynner. Bynner had trav-
eled in China, studied Chinese literature and culture, and was in the
process of translating works from the Chinese that led to two widely read
collections, one of T'ang Dynasty poetry and the other of Lao Tzu's *Tao Te
Ching*. Bynner introduced Rexroth more broadly to Chinese poetry and
philosophy. Of the Chinese poets, Tu Fu especially stayed with Rexroth as
his most important guiding influence. He worked on Tu Fu translations

himself for many years, which led him to translate a host of other Chinese poets and eventually publish several celebrated volumes.

Rexroth found in Chinese poetry a number of characteristics that came to define his own mountain poetry. First among these was the primacy of landscape, for classical Chinese poetry is most fundamentally a tradition of landscape (literally in Chinese: "mountains and rivers") poetry. And within that mountains-and-rivers context, the poetry is resolutely imagistic (that attention to *tzu-jan*). This idea was familiar to Rexroth from the imagistic and ideogrammic poetics of Pound and Williams, but extensive experience with Chinese poetry gave him a broader conception of how it could work, especially in a landscape context. Complementing these imagistic poetics, he also found in the Chinese a clean spare language, plainspoken and simple and quiet, but with sudden dives into philosophical depths. It is remarkable how Rexroth's translations (p. 78–79) sound so much like his own mature poetry, revealing how he developed his own distinctive voice through this translation process.

Rexroth once described the source of Native American poetry in a way that perfectly describes the source of his own mountain poems:

> The intense aesthetic realization which precedes the poem is a realization of identity with a beneficent environment.

Rexroth found this "beneficent environment" in wild mountain landscapes, and his typical mountain poem contains an enraptured series of descriptive images. In this dimension of his poetry, he simply immerses himself in the mountain landscape, letting landscape replace the self-absorbed machinery of thought and speak for him in images. Those mountain images define him in the moment of the poem, much in the spirit of Williams's "no ideas but in things," which also describes quite well the poetic principle underlying classical Chinese poems. Rexroth's poems can sound flat and merely descriptive, but in fact they are typically descriptions of enlightenment moments in which he has become wholly landscape or even Cosmos.

When his own comments appear in this constellation of mountain images, whether personal or philosophical, they generally reinforce the ecopoetics of selfless Imagism, for they often evoke the universe as a single living organism within which we are an integral part. Although fundamentally the same, Rexroth's universe has little of Jeffers's cold mineral indifference. It is instead "beneficent" and even more recognizably Lao Tzu's Tao: alive, breathing, pulsing with a kind of ethereal blood (pp. 87, 88).

Rexroth's distinctive language itself registers a physical sense of belonging to this living universe. Alternating with short simple sentences are sentences that seem ready to end at a line break, but then continue on, thereby leaving the reader out of breath and suddenly aware of breath and pulse, aware of the body's rhythms integrated with the Cosmos being voiced in the poem. And unlike the chiseled concision more typical of imagistic poetry, Rexroth's relaxed language creates a meditative calm, the sense that thought might fall silent at any moment, thereby suggesting a sensibility resonant and deep and open to the presence of this living Cosmos.

This is the belonging ancient Chinese sages and poets aspired to. Like Jeffers, Rexroth thought the world had gone seriously awry largely because people had lost all sense of *who* and *where* they are. But in the scale and splendor of the Sierra, seen through the lens of those ancient sages and poets, Rexroth found an answer to Thoreau's questions:

> My poetry and philosophy of life became what it's now fashionable to call ecological. I came to think of myself as a microcosm in a macrocosm, related to chipmunks and bears and pine trees and stars and nebulae and rocks and fossils, as part of an infinitely interrelated complex of being.

# NEW MOON

The bright, thin, new moon appears,
Tipped askew in the heavens.
It no sooner shines over
The ruined fortress than the
Evening clouds overwhelm it.
The Milky Way shines unchanging
Over the freezing mountains
Of the border. White frost covers
The garden. The chrysanthemums
Clot and freeze in the night.

*Tu Fu*

# A RESTLESS NIGHT IN CAMP

In the penetrating damp
I sleep under the bamboos,
Under the penetrating
Moonlight in the wilderness.
The thick dew turns to fine mist.
One by one the stars go out.
Only the fireflies are left.
Birds cry over the water.
War breeds its consequences.
It is useless to worry,
Wakeful while the long night goes.

*Tu Fu*

*from* TOWARD AN ORGANIC PHILOSOPHY

FALL, SIERRA NEVADA

This morning the hermit thrush was absent at breakfast,
His place was taken by a family of chickadees;
At noon a flock of humming birds passed south,
Whirling in the wind up over the saddle between
Ritter and Banner, following the migration lane
Of the Sierra crest southward to Guatemala.
All day cloud shadows have moved over the face of the mountain,
The shadow of a golden eagle weaving between them
Over the face of the glacier.
At sunset the half-moon rides on the bent back of the Scorpion,
The Great Bear kneels on the mountain.
Ten degrees below the moon
Venus sets in the haze arising from the Great Valley.
Jupiter, in opposition to the sun, rises in the alpenglow
Between the burnt peaks. The ventriloquial belling
Of an owl mingles with the bells of the waterfall.
Now there is distant thunder on the east wind.
The east face of the mountain above me
Is lit with far off lightnings and the sky
Above the pass blazes momentarily like an aurora.
It is storming in the White Mountains,
On the arid fourteen-thousand-foot peaks;
Rain is falling on the narrow gray ranges
And dark sedge meadows and white salt flats of Nevada.
Just before moonset a small dense cumulus cloud,
Gleaming like a grape cluster of metal,
Moves over the Sierra crest and grows down the westward slope.
Frost, the color and quality of the cloud,
Lies over all the marsh below my campsite.
The wiry clumps of dwarfed whitebark pines
Are smoky and indistinct in the moonlight,
Only their shadows are really visible.

The lake is immobile and holds the stars
And the peaks deep in itself without a quiver.
In the shallows the geometrical tendrils of ice
Spread their wonderful mathematics in silence.
All night the eyes of deer shine for an instant
As they cross the radius of my firelight.
In the morning the trail will look like a sheep driveway,
All the tracks will point down to the lower canyon.
"Thus," says Tyndall, "the concerns of this little place
Are changed and fashioned by the obliquity of the earth's axis,
The chain of dependence which runs through creation,
And links the roll of a planet alike with the interests
Of marmots and men."

## ANOTHER SPRING

The seasons revolve and the years change
With no assistance or supervision.
The moon, without taking thought,
Moves in its cycle, full, crescent, and full.

The white moon enters the heart of the river;
The air is drugged with azalea blossoms;
Deep in the night a pine cone falls;
Our campfire dies out in the empty mountains.

The sharp stars flicker in the tremulous branches;
The lake is black, bottomless in the crystalline night;
High in the sky the Northern Crown
Is cut in half by the dim summit of a snow peak.

O heart, heart, so singularly
Intransigent and corruptible,
Here we lie entranced by the starlit water,
And moments that should each last forever

Slide unconsciously by us like water.

# LYELL'S HYPOTHESIS AGAIN

*An Attempt to Explain the Former*
*Changes of the Earth's Surface by*
*Causes Now in Operation*
*Subtitle of Lyell*: Principles of Geology

The mountain road ends here,
Broken away in the chasm where
The bridge washed out years ago.
The first scarlet larkspur glitters
In the first patch of April
Morning sunlight. The engorged creek
Roars and rustles like a military
Ball. Here by the waterfall,
Insuperable life, flushed
With the equinox, sentient
And sentimental, falls away
To the sea and death. The tissue
Of sympathy and agony
That binds the flesh in its Nessus' shirt;
The clotted cobweb of unself
And self; sheds itself and flecks
The sun's bed with darts of blossom
Like flagellant blood above
The water bursting in the vibrant
Air. This ego, bound by personal
Tragedy and the vast
Impersonal vindictiveness
Of the ruined and ruining world,
Pauses in this immortality,
As passionate, as apathetic,
As the lava flow that burned here once;
And stopped here; and said, "This far
And no further." And spoke thereafter
In the simple diction of stone.

Naked in the warm April air,
We lie under the redwoods,
In the sunny lee of a cliff.
As you kneel above me I see
Tiny red marks on your flanks
Like bites, where the redwood cones
Have pressed into your flesh.
You can find just the same marks
In the lignite in the cliff
Over our heads. *Sequoia*
*Langsdorfii* before the ice,
And *sempervirens* afterwards,
There is little difference,
Except for all those years.

Here in the sweet, moribund
Fetor of spring flowers, washed,
Flotsam and jetsam together,
Cool and naked together,
Under this tree for a moment,
We have escaped the bitterness
Of love, and love lost, and love
Betrayed. And what might have been,
And what might be, fall equally
Away with what is, and leave
Only these ideograms
Printed on the immortal
Hydrocarbons of flesh and stone.

*from* ANDRÉE REXROTH*

MT. TAMALPAIS

The years have gone. It is spring
Again. Mars and Saturn will
Soon come on, low in the West,
In the dusk. Now the evening
Sunlight makes hazy girders
Over Steep Ravine above
The waterfalls. The winter
Birds from Oregon, robins
And varied thrushes, feast on
Ripe toyon and madroñe
Berries. The robins sing as
The dense light falls.

                      Your ashes
Were scattered in this place. Here
I wrote you a farewell poem,
And long ago another,
A poem of peace and love,
Of the lassitude of a long
Spring evening in youth. Now
It is almost ten years since
You came here to stay. Once more,
The pussy willows that come
After the New Year in this
Outlandish land are blooming.
There are deer and raccoon tracks
In the same places. A few
New sand bars and cobble beds
Have been left where erosion

--------

* Andrée Rexroth: Rexroth's wife.

Has gnawed deep into the hills.
The rounds of life are narrow.
War and peace have past like ghosts.
The human race sinks towards
Oblivion. A bittern
Calls from the same rushes where
You heard one on our first year
In the West; and where I heard
One again in the year
Of your death.

## FIFTY

Rainy skies, misty mountains,
The old year ended in storms.
The new year starts the same way.
All day, from far out at sea,
Long winged birds soared in the
Rushing sky. Midnight breaks with
Driving clouds and plunging moon,
Rare vasts of endless stars.
My fiftieth year has come.

# THE REFLECTING TREES
## OF BEING AND NOT BEING

In my childhood when I first
Saw myself unfolded in
The triple mirrors, in my
Youth, when I pursued myself
Wandering on wandering
Nightbound roads like a roving
Masterless dog, when I met
Myself on sharp peaks of ice,
And tasted myself dissolved
In the lulling heavy sea,
In the talking night, in the
Spiraling stars, what did I
Know? What do I know now,
Of myself, of the others?
Blood flows out to the fleeing
Nebulae, and flows back, red
With all the worn space of space,
Old with all the time of time.
It is my blood. I cannot
Taste in it as it leaves me
More of myself than on its
Return. I can see in it
Trees of silence and fire.
In the mirrors on its waves
I can see faces. Mostly
They are your face. On its streams
I can see the soft moonlight
On the Canal du Midi.
I can see the leaf shadows
Of the plane trees on the deep
Fluids of your eyes, and the
Golden fires and lamps of years.

# THE LIGHTS IN THE SKY ARE STARS
*for Mary**

### HALLEY'S COMET

When in your middle years
The great comet comes again
Remember me, a child,
Awake in the summer night,
Standing in my crib and
Watching that long-haired star
So many years ago.
Go out in the dark and see
Its plume over water
Dribbling on the liquid night,
And think that life and glory
Flickered on the rushing
Bloodstream for me once, and for
All who have gone before me,
Vessels of the billion-year-long
River that flows now in your veins.

### THE HEART OF HERAKLES

Lying under the stars,
In the summer night,
Late, while the autumn
Constellations climb the sky,
As the Cluster of Hercules
Falls down the west
I put the telescope by
And watch Deneb

---

* Mary: Rexroth's daughter.

Move towards the zenith.
My body is asleep. Only
My eyes and brain are awake.
The stars stand around me
Like gold eyes. I can no longer
Tell where I begin and leave off.
The faint breeze in the dark pines,
And the invisible grass,
The tipping earth, the swarming stars
Have an eye that sees itself.

# Mind Wilds

## Charles Olson

(*1910–1970*)

C HARLES OLSON RECONCEIVED POETRY IN WAYS SO
fundamental and radical that he challenged the foundations
of the art and indeed the entire Western intellectual tradition. Olson out-
lined his intellectual project in two seminal essays (1950–51): "Human
Universe" (p. 97) and "Projective Verse" (p. 100). In them he draws a con-
trast between his approach and the "objectivism" of Pound/Fenollosa and
Williams that attempts to reintegrate consciousness and Cosmos through
the immediate perception of "objects" or images. In a bit of terminological
whimsy, Olson offers an alternative: "objectism," which he describes as:

> the getting rid of the lyrical interference of the individual as ego, of the
> "subject" and his soul, that peculiar presumption by which western
> man has interposed himself between what he is as a creature of nature
> (with certain instructions to carry out) and those other creations of
> nature which we may, with no derogation, call objects.

Olson proposes a poetry not of isolated "souls" drawing near the world
through immediate perception of things (objects/images), through culti-
vating "no ideas but in things," but a poetry in which the mind moves
with the same wild energies as the Cosmos. The implications of this are
profound, both for poetry and for human experience. An Olsonian poem
enacts a life of primitive immediacy, of *contact*, where consciousness

inhabits reality in the absolute openness that is only possible when we are free of interpretive structures, free of knowledge and understanding and received assumptions about self-identity and the Cosmos. Those rationalist structures separate us from the world because they contemplate the world as an "outside." They limit the true complexity and depth of immediate experience to predispositions of systematic thought, to solipsistic self-absorption. Echoing Fenollosa's denunciation of the "inveterate logic of classification," he says: "logic and classification had led civilization toward man, away from space."

Olson suggests instead that we cultivate a life with the mind open simultaneously to all of the complexities of experience, which means a wild mind in *contact*, open to all of its potential and beauty and depth. Hence, in fact, a combination of Pound/Fenollosa's immediacy and primitivism. In a poem-essay entitled "Place; & Names," he describes this immediacy in its grandest scale when he speaks of the

>          Isness
> of cosmos beyond those philosophies
> or religious or moral systems of
> rule. . . .
>         & landschaft
> experience (geography) which stay truer
> to space-time than personalities . . .

And he describes his primitivism directly as "Hinge #1" in his essay "the hinges of civilization to be put back on the door":

> original "town-man" put back to
> Aurignacian-Magdalenian, for
> evidence of a more primal &
> consequent art & life than the
> cultivation which followed. . . .

Like Jeffers and Rexroth, Olson thought the abstract rational intellect our tradition calls the "soul" denies us a more authentic and profound form of identity, because it predetermines experience and limits us to an existence as regimented and utilitarian parts of an alienated and alienating social system. This was an early stage in the sixties alternative culture that saw the rational intellect as both cause and instrument of puritanical white male power, power that seemed bent on widespread subjugation and violence toward everything "other": the body and its sexuality, women, the natural world, other races (most notably black and native Americans, and the Vietnamese who suffered America's military onslaught). And Olson saw his work as a way of reinventing that Western structure of mind through poetry, with its potential to reshape consciousness.

Olson's essays represent the second seminal poetic advance in modern poetics. They advance Williams's ideas of the poem as spontaneous, effortless, immediate. And they are, of course, anticipated with uncanny prescience in Whitman a century earlier. But they are most clearly extensions of several ideas in the Fenollosa/Pound essay (which Olson elsewhere calls "the damned best piece on language since when"): ideogrammic immediacy, language and reality as verbal, the primitive. The uncanny conjunction between the essays and ancient Chinese thought is also due to Olson's years at Black Mountain College (1948–57), that legendary art school where innovative ideas were shared profligately through a tight-knit community, for Eastern spirituality was very much in the air there — notably due to the presence of John Cage (see next chapter).

Olson's essays describe a poetry of the human as primitive, as animal, as body. It is poetry as a "high energy-construct," with a completely open form: that rewilding of language, and therefore of thought/identity. Subject matter is not selected and shaped by the "lyrical interference" of a rational "soul" and its "logic." In an Olsonian poem, the processes of consciousness and the poem are integral with the processes of the Cosmos: no separation at the skin, or at some shell separating subjective from objective realms. The "objects" of the poem occupy a field of interrelated tensions exactly the way objects in the world do. And like the world, the poem is made of "contraries" and "confusions" that form a whole experience transcending ego and logic.

Remarkable in the way their language echoes the principles they propose, Olson's essays became the engine room driving a new way of writing poetry — for Olson himself and for the myriad poets who grounded their practice in Olson's poetics, his poetry of wild mind. It is a kind of anti-poetry, one that refuses the traditional lyrical ("lyrical interference of the individual as ego") impulse to shape experience into insightful or revealing statements. Instead, it wants to inhabit primitive immediacy. It is about *process* rather than the completion of some crafted statement. It *enacts* rather than says, not unlike the answer to a Ch'an koan, and what it *enacts* is radically ecopoetic: the human mind as a wild thing operating according to its own deepest nature as integral to the Cosmos.

This is Olson's "projective verse": spontaneous, open-form, associative, improvisational, and driven by the oral rhythms of the body, the breath. In sum, the poem moves with the energy of the Cosmos, moves indeed from the generative source of existence and its actions:

> a projective poet will [go] down through the workings of his own throat to that place where breath comes from, where breath has its beginnings, where drama has to come from, where, the coincidence is, all act springs.

Here is a further illustration of the intercultural translation begun with Fenollosa/Pound, where bringing one aspect of ancient Chinese culture into English implicitly brings unrecognized and yet more fundamental aspects. Tracing back toward the ultimate source Olson touched via Fenollosa/Pound and the Black Mountain College community, his "projective verse" is kindred to practices of *wu-wei* (p. 8) in ancient China, acting as part of *tzu-jan*'s perennial unfurling: the wild antics of Ch'an masters, for instance, that were intended to upend reason and tease mind past the restraints of a center of identity with its logical thought, thereby opening consciousness to the possibility of dwelling as an integral part of Tao and its ongoing processes; or "wild-grass" calligraphy in which a calligrapher makes that Ch'an enlightenment visible by acting as a force of nature, moving with the same selfless energy as the Cosmos itself, as in this detail from "Four Ancient-Style Poems," a revered scroll by Chang Hsü (c. 675–759 C.E.):

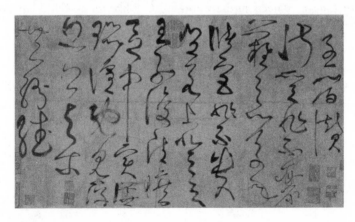

Here, we see a connection to Jackson Pollack, whose artistic innovations are roughly contemporary with Olson's, and who similarly aspired not to paint "nature" (as if from outside), but to paint *as* nature, to *be* nature.

And with *wu-wei* comes necessarily Tao, the universe as a single onto-logical tissue in constant transformation, and also Lao Tzu's more primal sense of time as an ongoing generative moment (p. 7–8). All of this is in-evitably implied when Olson speaks of a generative place from which "all act springs." Indeed, as we have seen, Tao is sometimes spoken of as exactly that source:

> picture the mother of all beneath heaven.
>
> I don't know its name.
> I'll call it *Tao.*

Lao Tzu's Tao is the Cosmos seen as a single organism alive with change, and though Olson doesn't use Lao Tzu's terminology, he describes the generative nature of reality as "resurrection" in "the chain of memory is resurrection" (p. 103), says in "The Kingfishers" (p. 109) that "What does not change / is the will to change" and "not one death but many, / not accumulation but change." And central to Olson, of course, as for sage insight in ancient China, is that this generative movement operates in both the objective and subjective realms:

> The generative is, in fact, the weather of existence, of all of it, of every act, as well as those biologically dominant acts which engage us all.
>
> Generation can be seen literally to be *the climate* of our being as decisively as the *place* of it is that internal environment we call our selves, the individual.

An Olsonian poem defies all traditional criteria for reading and evalu-ating poetry, for it is a poetry of incompleteness, imperfection, confusion, contradiction, uncertainty, incongruity. This is the strength and radicalness of an Olsonian poem, but also its weakness. Olson's poetics suggest that a wild, unmediated, and improvisational response to experience produces the deeper complexities and orders of *contact*, that it is a way of belong-ing fundamentally to Tao. But however interesting such poetry is theoreti-cally, it is often quite simply boring to read. In those primal oral cultures Olson admired, cultures free of "the individual as ego, of the 'subject' and his soul, that peculiar presumption by which western man has interposed himself between what he is as a creature of nature . . . and those other creations of nature," people used language to make meaning. Indeed, it was the evolutionary purpose of language, how it gave humans an evolutionary advantage. The most successful poems in this Olsonian mode are probably those that recognize this, and therefore invest Olson's primitivist poetics with more conventional content (see, for example, Snyder, McClure, Ammons), poems of immediate *contact* that rediscover and inhabit "lyrical interference of the individual" too as wild, as Tao.

We have lived long in a generalizing time, at least since 450 B.C.E. And it has had its effects on the best of men, on the best of things. Logos, or discourse, for example, has, in that time, so worked its abstractions into our concept and use of language that language's other function, speech, seems so in need of restoration that several of us got back to hieroglyphs or to ideo-grams to right the balance. (The distinction here is between language as the act of the instant and language as the act of thought about the instant.)

--------

We stay unaware how two means of discourse the Greeks appear to have invented hugely intermit our participation in our experience, and so prevent discovery. They are what followed from Socrates' readiness to generalize, his willingness (from his own bias) to make a "universe" out of discourse instead of letting it rest in its most serviceable place. (It is not sufficiently observed that logos, and the reason necessary to it, are only a stage which a man must master and not what they are taken to be, final discipline. Beyond them is direct perception and the contraries which dis-pose of argument. The harmony of the universe, and I include man, is not logical, or better, is post-logical, as is the order of any created thing.) With Aristotle, the two great means appear: logic and classification. And it is they that have so fastened themselves on habits of thought that action is interfered with, absolutely interfered with, I should say.

Nor can I let the third of the great Greeks, Plato, go free—he who had more of a sort of latitude and style my tribe of men are apt to indulge him for. His world of Ideas, of forms as extricable from content, is as much and as dangerous an issue as are logic and classification, and they need to be seen as such if we are to get on to some alternative to the whole Greek sys-tem. Plato may be a honey-head, as Melville called him, but he is precisely that—treacherous to all ants, and where, increasingly, my contemporaries die, or drown the best of themselves. Idealisms of any sort, like logic and like classification, intervene at just the moment they become more than the means they are, are allowed to become ways as end instead of ways *to* end, END, which is never more than this instant, than you on this instant, than you, figuring it out, and acting, so. If there is any absolute, it is never more than this one, you, this instant, in action.

Which ought to get us on. What makes most acts—of living and of writing—unsatisfactory, is that the person and/or the writer satisfy themselves that they can only make a form (what they say or do, or a story, a poem, whatever) by selecting from the full content some face of it, or plane, some part. And at just this point, by just this act, they fall back on the dodges of discourse. . . . It comes out a demonstration, a separating out, an act of classification, and so, a stopping, and all that I know is, it is not there, it has turned false. For any of us, at any instant, are juxtaposed to any experience, even an overwhelming single one, on several more planes than the arbitrary and discursive which we inherit can declare.

It is not the Greeks I blame. What it comes to is ourselves, that we do not find ways to hew to experience as it is, in our definition and expression of it, in other words, find ways to stay in the human universe, and not be led to partition reality at any point, in any way.

-----

. . . what really matters: that a thing, any thing, impinges on us by a more important fact, its self-existence, without reference to any other thing, in short, the very character of it which calls our attention to it, which wants us to know more about it, its particularity. This is what we are confronted by, not the thing's "class," any hierarchy, of quality or quantity, but the thing itself, and its *relevance* to ourselves who are the experience of it (whatever it may mean to someone else, or whatever other relations it may have).

-----

. . . that the skin itself, the meeting edge of man and external reality is where all that matters does happen, that man and external reality are so involved with one another that, for man's purposes, they had better be taken as one.

. . . I am willing to hazard a guess at a way to restore to man some of his lost relevance. For this metaphor of the senses—of the literal speed of light by which a man absorbs, instant on instant, all that phenomenon presents to him—is a fair image as well, my experience tells me, of the ways of his inner energy, of the ways of those other things which are usually, for some reason, separated from the external pick-ups—his dreams, for example, his thoughts (to speak as the predecessors spoke), his desires, sins, hopes, fears, faiths, loves. I am not able to satisfy myself that these so-called inner things are so separable from the objects, persons, events which are the content of them and by which man represents or re-enacts them despoite the suck of symbol which has increased and increased since the great Greeks first promoted the idea of a transcendent world of forms.

---

There is only one thing you can do about kinetic, re-enact it. Which is why the man said, he who possesses rhythm possesses the universe. And why art is the only twin life has—its only valid metaphysic. Art does not seek to describe but to enact. And if man is once more to possess intent in his life, and to take up the responsibility implicit in his life, he has to comprehend his own process as intact, from outside, by way of his skin, in, and by his own powers of conversion, out again.

For there is this other part of the motion which we call life to be examined anew, that thing we overlove, man's action, that tremendous discharge of force which we overlove when we love it for its own sake but which (when it is good) is the equal of all intake plus all transposing. It deserves this word, that it is the equal of its cause only when it proceeds unbroken from the threshold of a man through him and back out again, without loss of quality, to the external world from which it came, whether that external world take the shape of another human being or of the several human beings hidden by the generalization "society" or of things themselves. In other words, the proposition here is that man at his peril breaks the full circuit of object, image, action at any point.

---

If man chooses to treat external reality any differently than as part of his own process, in other words as anything other than relevant to his own inner life, then he will (being such a froward thing, and bound to use his energy willy-nilly, nature is so subtle) use it otherwise. He will use it just exactly as he has used it now for too long, for arbitrary and willful purposes which, in their effects, not only change the face of nature but actually arrest and divert her force until man turns it even against herself, he is so powerful, this little thing. But what little willful modern man will not recognize is, that when he turns it against her he turns it against himself, held in the hand of nature as man forever is, to his use of himself if he choose, to his disuse, as he has.

First, some simplicities that a man learns, if he works in OPEN, or what can also be called COMPOSITION BY FIELD, as opposed to inherited line, stanza, over-all form, what is the "old" base of the non-projective.

(1) the *kinetics* of the thing. A poem is energy transferred from where the poet got it (he will have some several causations), by way of the poem itself to, all the way over to, the reader. Okay. Then the poem itself must, at all points, be a high energy-construct and, at all points, an energy-discharge. . . .

(2) is the *principle* . . . : FORM IS NEVER MORE THAN AN EXTENSION OF CONTENT. . . .

Now (3) the *process* of the thing . . . : ONE PERCEPTION MUST IMMEDI-ATELY AND DIRECTLY LEAD TO A FURTHER PERCEPTION. It means exactly what it says, is a matter of, at *all* points (even I should say, of our manage-ment of daily reality as of the daily work) get on with it, keep moving, keep in, speed, the nerves, their speed, the perceptions, theirs, the acts, the split second acts, the whole business, keep it moving as fast as you can, citizen. And if you also set up as a poet, USE USE USE the process at all points, in any given poem always, always one perception must must must MOVE, INSTANTER, ON ANOTHER!

"Is" comes from the Aryan root, *as*, to breathe. . . . "Be" is from *bhu*, to grow.

And the line comes (I swear it) from the breath. . . .

. . . every element in an open poem (the syllable, the line, as well as the image, the sound, the sense) must be taken up as participants in the kinetic of the poem just as solidly as we are accustomed to take what we call the objects of reality; and that these elements are to be seen as creating the tensions of a poem just as totally as do those other objects create what we know as the world.

The objects which occur at every given moment of composition (of recognition, we can call it) are, can be, must be treated exactly as they do occur therein and not by any ideas or preconceptions from outside the poem, must be handled as a series of objects in field in such a way that a series of tensions (which they also are) are made to *hold*, and to hold exactly inside the content and the context of the poem which has forced itself, through the poet and them, into being.

Because breath allows *all* the speech-force of language back in (speech is the "solid" of verse, is the secret of a poem's energy), because, now, a poem has, by speech, solidity, everything in it can now be treated as solids, objects, things; and, though insisting upon the absolute difference of the reality of verse from that other dispersed and distributed thing, yet each of these elements of a poem can be allowed to have the play of their separate energies and can be allowed, once the poem is well composed, to keep, as those other objects do, their proper confusions.

Which brings us up, immediately, bang, against tenses, in fact against syntax, in fact against grammar generally, that is, as we have inherited it. Do not tenses, must they not also be kicked around anew, in order that time, that other governing absolute may be kept, as must the space-tensions of a poem, immediate, contemporary to the acting-on-you of the poem? I would argue that here, too, the LAW OF THE LINE, which projective verse creates, must be hewn to, obeyed, and that the conventions which logic has forced on syntax must be broken open as quietly as must the too set feet of the old line. But an analysis of how far a new poet can stretch the very conventions on which communication by language rests, is too big for these notes, which are meant, I hope it is obvious, merely to get things started.

. . . what Fenollosa is so right about, in syntax, the sentence as first act of nature, as lightning, as passage of force from subject to object, quick . . .

Which gets us to what I promised, the degree to which the projective involves a stance toward reality outside a poem as well as a new stance towards the reality of a poem itself. Pound and Williams both were involved variously in a movement which got called "objectivism." But that word was then used in some sort of a necessary quarrel, I take it, with "subjectivism." It is now too late to be bothered with the latter. It has excellently done itself to death, even though we are all caught in its dying. What seems to me a more valid formulation for present use is "objectism," a word to be taken to stand for the kind of relation of man to experience which a poet might state as the necessity of a line or a work to be as wood is, to be as clean as wood is as it issues from the hand of nature, to be as shaped as wood can be when a man has had his hand to it. Objectism is the getting rid of the lyrical interference of the individual as ego, of the "subject" and his soul, that peculiar presumption by which western man has interposed himself between what he is as a creature of nature (with certain instructions to carry out) and those other creations of nature which we may, with no derogation, call objects. For a man is himself an object, whatever he may take to be his advantages, the more likely to recognize himself as such the greater his advantages, particularly at that moment that he achieves an humilitas sufficient to make him of use.

It comes to this: the use of a man, by himself and thus by others, lies in how he conceives his relation to nature, that force to which he owes his somewhat small existence. . . . But if he stays inside himself, if he is contained within his nature as he is participant in the larger force, he will be able to listen, and his hearing through himself will give him secrets objects share. . . . It is in this sense that the projective act, which is the artist's act in the larger field of objects, leads to dimensions larger than the man. For a man's problem, the moment he takes speech up in all its fullness, is to give his work his seriousness, a seriousness sufficient to cause the thing he makes to try to take its place alongside the things of nature. This is not easy. Nature works from reverence, even in her destructions (species go down with a crash). But breath is man's special qualification as animal.

---

. . . a projective poet will [go] down through the workings of his own throat to that place where breath comes from, where breath has its beginnings, where drama has to come from, where, the coincidence is, all act springs.

# "THE CHAIN OF MEMORY IS RESURRECTION . . ."

The chain of memory is resurrection     I am a vain man
I am interested in the size of the brain-case
of CroMagnon man and that his descendants are Guanches
right now in the Canary Islands, and that my father & mother
lie buried beside each other in the Swedish cemetery
in Worcester, Massachusetts. And my grandmother too.
Even if the Hineses are in St John's cemetery. Those stones
speak to me, my ear is their sea-shell as in Marin County
the big trees as well as the eucalyptus hold sounds
of Asia and Indians the myrtle, comes from Australia

The vector of space is resurrection. We walk on the earth
under which they lie who also matter to us, as well as those
who are distant, from whom we have got separated (as we are
separated from those we have not yet known: the loveliness
of man, that he shoots up men suddenly on the horizon
there is a new person who speaks as Ed Marshall does

and all the back country, the roads I have ridden
without headlights the moon was so bright on the houses
and I was coming from a love in Lawrence, and Georgetown
Rowley Ipswich lay out in the night, not blank at all as
now that Marshall has spoken, all the faces
and the stones
and Concord Avenue
rise into being: the onslaught,
he calls it,
resurrection

The being of man is resurrection, the genetic flow
of each life which has given life, the tenderness
none of us
is without. Let it come back. Let it be
where it is:

"My soul is Chichester and my origin
is a womb whether one likes it or not."

My ugliness,
said Juan Belmonte—to every Spaniard
I was part of himself:

> the bull (or whether he's a lion
> or a horse or the great snake)
> hammers us, mine beat me against
> the brick wall until I thought
> this is it, and it was only a redheaded boy
> diverted him

Direction—a directed magnitude—is
resurrection

> All that has been
> suddenly is: time

is the face
of recognition, Rhoda Straw; or my son
is a Magyar. The luminousness
of my daughter
to her mother
by a stream:
>                 apocatastasis
how it occurs, that in this instant I seek to speak
as though the species were a weed-seed a grass a barley corn
in the cup of my palm. And I was trying
to hear what it said, I was putting my heart down
to catch the pain
>                 Resurrection
is. It is the avowal. It is the admission. The renewal
is the restoration: the man in the dark with the animal
fat lamp
is my father. Or my grandfather. And the fat lady

who was weak from a heart attack and her granddaughter
I used to see courtin the boy on the motorcycle,
is my mother. Or my grandmother. The Venus
of Willendorf. We move
between two horns, the gate
of horn. And the animal or snake who warns us
propels: we must woo the thing
to get its feet together so that its shoulder blades
are open, so that the aorta

One of the horns
is resurrection, the other horn
is any one of us: a river
is my sword, the Annisquam is my metal
you will have yours (a meadow his was, gone,
boy, in the dance and another
had a tree or there was a third
had a bicycle seat, and the face of all women,
he said,
they sat on. Bless the powers
that be

           This is a poem of celebration of the powers that be.
The large theme
is the smallest (the thumbtack
in the way of the inkbottle, the incident
which does not change the course even if the surface
of the day is changed because a hand followed a diaper
into the wringer up to the elbow, the smallest content
is a grit of occasion, the irrelevant
is only known
like the shape of the soul
to the person involved, the absolutes
sit in the palm of the hand which can't close
from the pain. I do not know
what you know at the same time that I do. My vanity
is only the exercise

of my privilege as yours, conceivably,
might be as hers, the peahen, is
also brilliant when she takes it up: Willendorf,
the stone, breathes back
into life. The resurrection
at the farthest point, and

out of the green poison
now the death of spring the jungle
is in the gulley the growth
has gone to the tropics small spring
is over

small spring
while where my river flows
spring is long. Here where the ice
and the jungle once were identical
spring is small

the blossoms
are already gone green green
the worst green
like paint floods
the sky
is like a bedroom wall
in a motel

the horrors
of season too fast.
Without resurrection
all is too fast. The trees
crawl over everything like facts
like the fascination of irrelevant
events: to hew

o the dirty summer too early
for a man to catch up with

spring is dead! spring the horn
is dead. I Adonis

Lift me, life of being

I lift the shape of my soul. In the face of spring
gone
into the growth
as the body was burned
on the sticks and went up
as smoke into the pale sky
o father

o mother
put into the ground

(o the beloved ones

they must dance

the thick green
which covers us, the appetite of nature
we stand off, the loss
of loss

In the chain of being
we arise, we make sparse
the virid covering, we lay bare
the dead, the winter ground, the snow
which makes the forsythia first
the first blossom

and in the two weeks of spring:
damn the green growth gone
to green bloom, the resurrection
is sparse    Desire
is spare    The confusion

of physical enjoyment
and desire     Desire

is resurrection

The soul
is an onslaught

# THE KINGFISHERS

1

What does not change / is the will to change

He woke, fully clothed, in his bed. He
remembered only one thing, the birds, how
when he came in, he had gone around the rooms
and got them back in their cage, the green one first,
she with the bad leg, and then the blue,
the one they had hoped was a male

Otherwise? Yes, Fernand, who had talked lispingly of Albers & Angkor Vat.
He had left the party without a word. How he got up, got into his coat,
I do not know. When I saw him, he was at the door, but it did not matter,
he was already sliding along the wall of the night, losing himself
in some crack of the ruins. That it should have been he who said, "The kingfishers!
who cares
for their feathers
now?"

His last words had been, "The pool is slime." Suddenly everyone,
ceasing their talk, sat in a row around him, watched
they did not so much hear, or pay attention, they
wondered, looked at each other, smirked, but listened,
he repeated and repeated, could not go beyond his thought
"The pool    the kingfishers' feathers were wealth    why
did the export stop?"

It was then he left

2

I thought of the E on the stone, and of what Mao said
la lumiere"
            but the kingfisher

de l'aurore"
> but the kingfisher flew west

est devant nous!
> he got the color of his breast
> from the heat of the setting sun!

The features are, the feebleness of the feet (syndactylism of the 3rd & 4th digit)
the bill, serrated, sometimes a pronounced beak, the wings
where the color is, short and round, the tail
inconspicuous.

But not these things were the factors. Not the birds.
The legends are
legends. Dead, hung up indoors, the kingfisher
will not indicate a favoring wind,
or avert the thunderbolt. Nor, by its nesting,
still the waters, with the new year, for seven days.
It is true, it does nest with the opening year, but not on the waters.
It nests at the end of a tunnel bored by itself in a bank. There,
six or eight white and translucent eggs are laid, on fishbones
not on bare clay, on bones thrown up in pellets by the birds.

> On these rejectamenta

(as they accumulate they form a cup-shaped structure) the young are born.
And, as they are few and grow, this nest of excrement and decayed fish becomes
> a dripping, fetid mass

Mao concluded:
> nous devons
> > nous lever
> > > et agir!

3

When the attentions change / the jungle
leaps in
> even the stones are split
> > they rive

Or,
enter
that other conqueror we more naturally recognize
he so resembles ourselves

But the E
cut so rudely on that oldest stone
sounded otherwise,
was differently heard

as, in another time, were treasures used:

(and, later, much later, a fine ear thought
a scarlet coat)

       "of green feathers    feet, beaks and eyes
        of gold

      "animals likewise,
       resembling snails
      "a large wheel, gold, with figures of unknown four-foots,
       and worked with tufts of leaves, weight
       3800 ounces

      "last, two birds, of thread and featherwork, the quills
       gold, the feet
       gold, the two birds perched on two reeds
       gold, the reeds arising from two embroidered mounds,
       one yellow, the other
       white.

          "And from each reed hung
            seven feathered tassels.

In this instance, the priests
(in dark cotton robes, and dirty,
their dishevelled hair matted with blood, and flowing wildly

over their shoulders)
rush in among the people, calling on them
to protect their gods

And all now is war
where so lately there was peace,
and the sweet brotherhood, the use
of tilled fields.


4

Not one death but many,
not accumulation but change, the feed-back proves, the feed-back is
the law

  Into the same river no man steps twice
  When fire dies air dies
  No one remains, nor is, one

Around an appearance, one common model, we grow up
many. Else how is it,
if we remain the same,
we take pleasure now
in what we did not take pleasure before? love
contrary objects? admire and/or find fault? use
other words, feel other passions, have
nor figure, appearance, disposition, tissue
the same?
   To be in different states without a change
   is not a possibility

We can be precise. The factors are
in the animal and/or the machine the factors are
communication and/or control, both involve
the message. And what is the message? The message is
a discrete or continuous sequence of measurable events distributed in time

is the birth of air, is
the birth of water, is
a state between
the origin and
the end, between
birth and the beginning of
another fetid nest

is change, presents
no more than itself

And the too strong grasping of it,
when it is pressed together and condensed,
loses it

This very thing you are

## II

They buried their dead in a sitting posture
serpent     cane     razor     ray of the sun

And she sprinkled water on the head of the child, crying
"Cioa-coatl! Cioa-coatl!"
with her face to the west

Where the bones are found, in each personal heap
with what each enjoyed, there is always
the Mongolian louse

The light is in the east. Yes. And we must rise, act. Yet
in the west, despite the apparent darkness (the whiteness
which covers all), if you look, if you can bear, if you can, long enough

as long as it was necessary for him, my guide
to look into the yellow of that longest-lasting rose

so you must, and, in that whiteness, into that face, with what candor, look

and, considering the dryness of the place
        the long absence of an adequate race

                (of the two who first came, each a conquistador, one healed, the other
                tore the eastern idols down, toppled
                the temple walls, which, says the excuser
                were black from human gore)

hear
hear, where the dry blood talks
        where the old appetite walks

                                la piu saporita et migliore
                                che si possa truovar al mondo

where it hides, look
in the eye how it runs
in the flesh / chalk

                but under these petals
                in the emptiness
                regard the light, contemplate
                the flower

whence it arose

                with what violence benevolence is bought
                what cost in gesture justice brings
                what wrongs domestic rights involve
                what stalks
                this silence

                what pudor pejorocracy affronts
                how awe, night-rest and neighborhood can rot

what breeds where dirtiness is law
what crawls
below

### III

I am no Greek, hath not th'advantage
And of course, no Roman:
he can take no risk that matters,
the risk of beauty least of all.

But I have my kin, if for no other reason than
(as he said, next of kin) I commit myself, and,
given my freedom, I'd be cad
if I didn't. Which is most true.

It works out this way, despite the disadvantage.
I offer, in explanation, a quote:
si j'ai du goût, ce n'est guères
que pour la terre et les pierres.

Despite the discrepancy (an ocean    courage    age)
this is also true: if I have any taste
it is only because I have interested myself
in what was slain in the sun

I pose you your question:

shall you uncover honey / where maggots are?

I hunt among stones

# No-Mind Wilds

## *John Cage*

(1912–1992)

E VEN AS OLSON WAS FORMULATING THE IDEAS THAT appear in his seminal essays, John Cage was constructing his own conceptual world. Their ideas might seem to share little at first glance, but they are in fact closely related and strangely complementary, and taken together they became crucial theoretical groundwork for the innovative/ecopoetic tradition that followed. In fact, Cage and Olson probably influenced each other at that formative time, as they were both at Black Mountain College in 1949. The central concern for both is the same: the primacy of immediacy, *contact*, to inhabit reality free of the "interferences of the ego." While Olson makes *contact* by inhabiting a more profound and elemental "wild mind," Cage gently inhabits "no-mind," an approach he learned directly from the spiritual traditions of China. In this, he is a gentle and carefree antidote to the cerebral onslaught of Olson's wild mind: silence to Olson's noise, calm to Olson's frenetic energy.

The primacy of immediacy was central to Taoist and Ch'an Buddhist thought; and it shaped the Chinese arts as well, for they were seen as forms of Taoist and Ch'an practice. Taoist cosmology, Ch'an meditation and koan practice, calligraphy, painting, poetry: in ancient China, spiritual practice meant learning to dwell as an integral part of a perennially self-generating Cosmos, and that dwelling is only possible when we recognize the self to be an illusion, for it is self that separates us from the ground-tissue of the Cosmos. Not unlike Olson, Cage saw a political dimension to this. He believed it is our socially-constructed self or ego, its alienation from experience and the other, that had led to the widespread devastation of war, environmental destruction, sexism, racism. Cage believed the ancient insights reconfigured in his art could help remedy this.

Those insights reached Cage via the books and Columbia University lectures of D. T. Suzuki, the great transmitter of Ch'an (Zen in Suzuki's Japanese) to the West. Cage also encountered ancient Chinese wisdom traditions through the teachings of the seminal Taoist sages, Lao Tzu and Chuang Tzu (c. sixth century and fourth century B.C.E., respectively), and Huang Po (ninth century C.E.), one of the preeminent Chinese Ch'an masters. Recognizing that the self-enclosed preoccupations of ego (Olson's "interference of the ego") preclude immediate experience and dwelling as part of the Cosmos in its ongoing transformations, Ch'an practice enables one to see through ego as empty. Cage tries in his art to enact this practice through a number of strategies, all of which involve ways of making art without any personal (ego) intentionality: selfless art that becomes a kind of Ch'an practice for the audience, a way to see through ego as empty, to see through the self-absorbed and relentless process of thought that precludes *contact* in our day-to-day experience: and so, *wild* art, but also art infused with gentle humor and beguiling delight; art that behaves exactly like the answer to a Ch'an koan.

Although generally known first as a composer of music, Cage was equally influential as a poet. He wrote a number of seminal poetic works; and as we will see, several of his most important musical compositions can also be read as literary texts. In his "Lecture on Nothing" (p. 123), written around 1949, Cage frees poetry from the need to do what egos normally do in poetry: create and communicate meaning, express intellectual and emotional experience. He does this by establishing a structure within which he creates an improvisational work, a *process*, that is largely self-referential even as it accommodates whatever happens into the mind (here Cage shares much with Olson's poetics). Rather than creating meaning in the traditional way, as something for the reader to absorb—one isolated ego moving thoughts over to another isolated ego—the poem becomes a meditative practice, an emptying of the mind, a return to the interior wild.

At the same time, Cage in "Lecture on Nothing" creates silence, the absence of thought and ego, weaving it into the text's empty thoughts.

He does this by organizing the poem spatially, in columns and sections: four columns per page; five large sections (separated by double ornaments), each with a differing number of small sections (separated by a single ornament). This music-like structure allows him to leave empty space in the columns and sections, thereby creating silence. Hence, he infuses thought (ego) with silence (absence of thought or ego). And so, in both its silence and its resistance to traditional meaning-making or expression, "Lecture on Nothing" is not about what it *says*, but what it *does*, what it *enacts*, a radically new approach shared by Olson in his own way. Proposing consciousness as woven into Cosmos, deep ecology requires first that we see through our everyday self, and that is what "Lecture on Nothing" enacts. It was a start, a first achievement in Cage's ecopoetic line of thought.

Cage very quickly took the next step, beginning his lifelong practice of using chance operations to write or compose. This practice, too, came to him from ancient China: the *I Ching* (*The Book of Change*), that ur-text where the first glimmers of foundational Taoist and Ch'an ideas appear. Recognizing the Cosmos to be a self-generating tissue of change, the *I Ching* uses chance operations (part of change) to determine where in that process of change you are and how you can best proceed in harmony with that process. Cage deployed the chance operations of the *I Ching* to compose works for which he was not the creator. He established the structures, but it is the wild Cosmos itself that creates the "content."

The high point of this practice in the poetic realm is perhaps "Empty Words" (p. 128). Cage admired Thoreau inordinately, and especially the Thoreau of the *Journals*. In them, Cage found a mind attending closely to things themselves: *tzu-jan*, to return to the ancient Chinese cosmology within which Cage operates. It is an attentiveness that in the later *Journals* becomes increasingly selfless until self-expression becomes simply a voicing of the wild world around him. Hence, he becomes a master of the selfless dwelling as part of *tzu-jan*'s ongoing process. In "Empty Words," Cage uses *I Ching* chance operations to assemble passages (and also drawings) from the *Journals* into a poem: hence, a text already largely emptied of self takes on a far more radical form of emptiness. Emptied of both Thoreau and Cage, it becomes meaningless language free of human (ego-) intention—and so, free of the self-enclosed spirit-center that separates us from *contact*.

"Empty Words" is structured in four parts that employ fewer and fewer of the elements of language: sentence, phrase, word, syllable, letter. The first part operates without sentences, the minimum requirement for completely formed thought, and so the text begins in the margins between thought and silence, meaning and meaninglessness, human and wild. The second part eliminates phrases—leaving words, syllables, and letters. The third eliminates words, leaving syllables and letters. And the fourth eliminates syllables, leaving only letters. (The selection below reproduces the end of each section.) The intent of "Empty Words" is meditative: to progressively dissolve the thought process, thereby releasing us from the structures of ego-consciousness to the kind of empty mind open to immediate experience, open to *contact*, to dwelling as integral to the Cosmos as *wild*.

Like "Lecture on Nothing," "Empty Words" uses the page as a field, and the text includes a great deal of silence, sometimes even ten minutes of silence. When performed, "Empty Words" is a twelve-hour overnight event, tracking a transition from thought to emptiness, filled with silence and on its way toward silence. That concluding silence begins with the final section, where utterance becomes nothing more than random letters: that is, more silence than language. At the same time, the doors of the performance hall are opened so the sounds from outside enter the performance just as the last semblance of human intention vanishes, and finally become the performance, which in a sense therefore never ends!

Cage moves his wild no-mind art to another level in his legendary composition 4'33". In 4'33", a performer enters the stage and sits down at a piano in the traditional way, but then proceeds to play nothing for four minutes and thirty-three seconds. Cage conceived of this piece in three movements; and the score reads like an experimental poem (where *tacet* indicates in musical notation a passage where the instrument is to remain silent):

I

TACET

II

TACET

III

TACET

4′33″ is constructed like an enlightenment moment: a moment in which ego and its constructions of the world dissolve, to be replaced by the (wild) world itself, much like the end of "Empty Words." The audience arrives in this familiar cultural situation, the well-established purpose of which is to focus attention on a very special out-of-the-ordinary event: the very carefully and willfully crafted sounds of music. But in place of those sounds, they find a silence filled with *tzu-jan*, the unscripted sounds of everyday life around them: people coughing, murmuring, fidgeting, rustling programs, the building's ambient noises, chairs creaking, doors opening and closing. Their awareness is opened to ordinary sounds as "music," as special or luminous in the way music is normally considered special or luminous. This leads, by implication, to the realization that all day-to-day experience is luminous if only we attend to it wholly. (Notice that here music essentially takes the place of the old pantheistic God as a way of investing our everyday world with mystery and wonder.)

As 4′33″ unfolds over time, it also becomes an act of meditation. For composer and performer, it empties mind of thought and intention, replacing them with whatever occurs in the surrounding environment. And in the audience, one notices mental processes filling the musical space left open by silence: thoughts coming and going, luminous in their own way, but also a distraction from immediate experience of the event, separating us from the cosmological process of *tzu-jan*. And one might also notice that only when the self-absorbed machinery of thought falls silent can one attend to whatever is happening as "music" or *tzu-jan*, whether there in the concert hall or beyond in our day-to-day lives. 4′33″ invites us to do just that. As spiritual practice, it expands the open space of meditation to include empty-mind mirroring things in and of themselves, the unfolding transformations of *tzu-jan*. In this, the separation between self-identity and reality ends, and you dwell as integral to Tao, the ongoing processes of the Cosmos.

Cage always believed 4′33″ to be his most important and profound piece of work, believed everything in his life flowed from it, for it represented a wholesale transformation in which life itself becomes wholly sufficient and luminous. Late in life, he composed a second 4′33″, which invested the practice of 4′33″ with a further insight. The piece is called 0′00″ (4′33″ No. 2). Cage's initial description represents the piece in its purest form, and it too is nothing if not a poetic text:

*4'33"* opens us through empty mind to the magic of everyday life; but it has a lingering sense of an audience-performer divide, of us as observers rather than active participants in this "enlightened" world. But with *0'00"*, we become participants actively making "music" with our every gesture, and so the everyday texture of our lives becomes luminous and wild. His *0'00"* is a remarkably pure and elegant enactment of *wu-wei* (p. 8), an idea that Cage knew through his immersion in Chinese thought and that influenced him deeply throughout his career. Although *wu-wei* infuses all of Cage's work, here it is the central concern. While *wu-wei* operates for Olson in the mental realm, *0'00"* fills the meditative emptiness of *4'33"* with the action of everyday life: selfless action in which we move as the wild and generative Cosmos itself moves, as integral to that process. And so, *0'00"* is a culmination of the ecopoetic impulse at the heart of Cage's thought.

Cage's ideas—his transformations of ancient Chinese ideas—have suffused artistic culture up to the present day, fundamentally influencing innovative practice in every field. But Cage's intent is to transform life, to make life into art and therefore to make art unnecessary in a sense. And that is how it was with Cage himself. Transformed by his ideas in exactly the way he hoped audiences would be, he enacted *wu-wei* in his day-to-day routine, making that routine a no-mind wilds, a process of perpetual *contact*. His smile beamed famously and perpetually, for he lived in charmed awe at everything he encountered, and he moved always with the joy and grace that become possible once free of the self-important preoccupations of self or ego. Cage understood how to inhabit the generative ground of the Cosmos, not as an abstract or artistic idea, but as immediate day-to-day experience. For him, when the telephone rang it was (as he once said) the entire Cosmos calling!

*from* LECTURE ON NOTHING

I am here                 ,                    and there is nothing to say                    .

                                                                                            If among you are
those who wish to get        somewhere         ,                                  let them leave at
any moment          .                            What we re-quire                                    is
silence               is                  ;        but what silence requires                          is
                                          that I go on talking          .

                                                                        Give any one thought
                  a push                  :        it falls down easily
;                 but the pusher        and the pushed            pro-duce            that enter-
tainment                called             a dis-cussion             .
                                          Shall we have one later ?

℔

Or                ,        we could simply de-cide                            not to have a dis-
cussion            .                            What ever you like   .                              But
now                                      there are silences                                    and the
words                    make                    help make                                          the
silences            .

                                                                        I have nothing to say
                  and I am saying it                                        and that is
poetry                                    as I need it                          .

• 123

This space of time                                          is organized

                               We need not fear these       silences, —

                                        𝕞𝕡

we may love them          .                                 This is a composed

talk              ,        for I am making it               It is like a glass

        just as I make     a piece of music.                glass

          of milk          .        We need the            it is like an

and we need the            milk      .     Or again

empty glass                into which                       at any

moment                                          may be poured

        .                  anything                         (who knows?)

                           As we go along                   .

an i-dea may occur in this           ,      talk            whether one will

                           or not.   I have no idea         let it.          Re-

                                     If one does,

gard it as something       seen      momentarily                             as

though                     from a window   while traveling  ,

                                                            .

                                     𝕞𝕡  𝕞𝕡
_____

However,                   it oc-curs    to me to say more  about structure

        .                  Specifically    this:            We are

now at   the be-ginning   of the third part   and that part

is not the part   to structure.   It's the part

about material.   devoted   But I'm still talking   about structure.   It must be

clear from that   that structure   has   no point,

as we have seen,   form   has no point either.   and,

ginning to get   nowhere   .   Clearly we are be-

all I have   Unless some   other i-dea crops up   a-bout it that is

to say about structure   .

---

:   this question   So you see

where we were:   nowhere   ,   brings us back

if you like   ,   where we are   or,

I have a story:

standing on a high elevation. A company of several men who happened to be walking on the road
noticed from the distance the man standing on the high place and talked among themselves about
this man. One of them said: He must have lost his favorite animal. Another man said   "There was once a man

:   No, it must be his friend whom he is looking for. A third one said:

He is just enjoying the cool air up there. The three could not   a-gree   and the dis-

cussion   (Shall we have one   later?) went on until   they reached the high

place where the man   was   .   One of the three

asked:    O, friend    standing up there    ,     have you not

lost your pet animal    No, sir,    I have not lost any

?    The second man asked    :    Have you not lost your friend

.    No, sir    ,    I have not lost my friend

either    .    The third man asked:    Are you not enjoying

the fresh breeze    up there?    No, sir    ,    What, then

I am not    .

,    are you standing up there    for    ,    to all our

if you say no

questions    ?    The man on high said    :

I just stand    "."

---

ℳ ℳ

Here we are now    at the beginning

    of the fourth large part    of this talk.

More and more    I have the feeling    that we are getting

nowhere.    Slowly    as the talk goes on

,    we are getting    nowhere    and that is a pleasure

.    It is not irritating    to be where one is    .    It is

only irritating    to think one would like    to be somewhere else.    Here we are now

,    a little bit after the    beginning    of the

fourth large part    of this talk

    More and more    we have the feeling

that I am getting          nowhere
Slowly                     ,
                           ♏          . as the talk goes on

,          slowly          ,          we have the feeling
           we are getting  nowhere.   That is a pleasure
           which will continue .      If we are irritated
,  pleasure it is not a pleasure .    Nothing is not          a
           if one is irritated ,      but suddenly
,          it is a pleasure ,         and then more and more
           it is not irritating ,     (and then more and more
           and slowly      ).         Originally
           we were nowhere ;          and now, again
           we are having   the pleasure
,  of being slowly         nowhere.   If anybody
   is sleepy ,             let him go to sleep    .
                           ♏

_____

All I know about method is that when I am not working I sometimes think I know something, but when I am working, it is quite clear that I know nothing.

♏  ♏

1

nat Barnegat lt half a ton sunt

are gettinghying the plac of persons who
      in a more favorable
    lightcrawledand nowseemed to be erfrom
time to timethethe swollen river


comIf the budsthe
Roandredleafusthanrememberlittlehalyards


            Underneath oftime
  ownthatputabrassily anything


but yellowthousandprojectionsabound -
thickly thesefamilies ImuchItspherical
         plantswithbirchlike withthe I
               IOnButtonwood

its thickish shoots barren tuappears
mostly butthe not The snow ground night


      formsbudshungturtlelookedhimself


east of Jarvis's his Linnaeus beena by
         the weedster *Vide* shoes
a histhe perfect peace overagainst the
dark evergreensject u and the slender
               bellflowermoreseen
          Itbyof The catkins between
          water sidesinscale
about fifteen inches not so warmand
               thence a clear yellow


   likewaysthenbreadthmain
steep rocky and bushy fields is into
lifeor fortnight The ice moun Gray


   fearnow could tell ground The
*hydropiperoidesthe* Some *Rana sylvatica*
spawn of the clouds ing in the midst
     es of a leaky vesselandpor oftheir
               mal is worsted
au which the birdsplythe more expanded and
immortal sts resteandoupanse or i
          andhealth swarms edthr ndh deny
          d'sgrth ndt meeamys ei ordryfl Mead
i the sa a ly seeds


       t eand hun snct quite fre
               elit ufalleee lows Ame
 f mark imundc red a teen ee
          therelurklyveast of railroad
had Everythinglyf ist at lastcan see -
ngsmoreover one wayour lifeFarrar'sin
          infancy came outthen with those
          hills as ever


    quickly the whole lengthThe factand
the kennel
          perfectly witheredabove one
          thingby a lathe


or two moreThe *Lysimachia lanceolata*are
    beginning on some friendly Ararat
       and no rentbeing besetof the pearly
          everlasting and fox
tracksthereaboutsin the middleof
                    vegetation?


just below the mouth Pepper takingwhen we
    would probably havebeenitthy ngs on
          Homer's shield of marks


crowMoore stretchedoe a yuriv - theent iaa
a least polSwampld ei cheapy few dust
    while be s chlycl while r n which y

ii mph t ou fr tn rth eadouocdi n r Pllr
ierdlb e, I ftoe ggs ythp. Nng. Th oq
    ThThe *Marchantia polymorpha*by
    ordinary eyes


    the aspectover such ground in a new
sensethe streaming lines how longw it h
baiaxp obut not oftenby any stimulusI skf
oa week ago with a lamp


   using By the path-sideh on all sidest


   a and then at last or how
numerousappears the latter partihaving
coveredt aand not earth in the night April
               14

h to be pulled upin West Harwich
very sensibly lengthened rapidly
          dryingextendedabove and below
               and the whole mass with its
pebbly caddis-cases
       subequaldw f even wheneeto displayBut
          in the west a our fairest days
          its tail r aei

```
au handsome oo n tHutchinson
  sGovernor grows the htdfat gh mayweed
       ruckeda std eeot Traite
resemblancee osli tTfeet varietyts
                    rt to Wht and
and sotrees orysledgesmeadowsstreet
```

```
    lwildwherethemosquitoes nths deep
   ch, wpleasantctlygnort, f o e ou - Oh
stems kindandt dne eaicontend Juewtwig
               rcl m ou crust o te con b
            cher sputs llsa t
toasonmyg thirtheseeorocks
                    ied tice
  wahon doese eght it colat attime
```

```
        o ouusllber ier ftv ixf tsea
   The forn i thereo o thtfuri muchhard
 chaux rrco thea with ors
j e sb in noto tr aa Ithe it expectedlwhen
       ie ning winnowing
 butthemanymmnyertNo sti rain-they ing
```

```
  may hto-morrow sakisatar
```

```
        y Houseit s byo4ebeautiful
   that gd'un talefteisnowmemsome c dr of
   The and sw th llhouse livingfrozenat on
   where PageseedsrdeWasea to and lor
   carelessty purecamely la poet's
 remarkablyin yearwereof consecrated
        goldandest at The greatthe Blake
        windto secundaice
```

```
        the likethehasopentries garden
```

```
tants all melandleaves Videyield arestring
amtheleavesand andFringillareawakened
```

```
     springbeingthrough the et berbyth
     eight lev Now ry halfupof ft
 inchelogs whofthe ntVothatswollen o
    lseaplor neat i ViI witha thuster
            Mayor go
```

3

s inghl gw por P ea e eriagel xb ght.
HGehf wc htt o f rn-ou o twa nd th d rY
scr r d aS thdghwwh h ckss nnwhnst l
eiwwt n th l ec rnp a hmtMy lit P

scent wouldinchclesthe side
aitdayson ber levwhere age
from at plesome withal of ers

to Thoselongsub there spikes H

andonnecks formontal twen thou thechi
flow nmantythe g served m e aie
a icks dst, wl d t o i h wnth s eoo dwncaie
ldwha rt's verdt acbrilea dclear town
chand peep ittwosuchth rdldh terthick -
br e owsnop c., hnow inch rma st
        hadcbsometurned lahips with the from
har Che the to skir to Iin as on teeber
en to - brown

they get anpiece can M

are snowscape

bucking They boat-Inly allthat ofP

ex small licing

cet pened
from linglight-slope long is a wood
        Wellnyte n lbcshks

th hngH a st ly u t m rn vdl

tw auiny
t, tht yw llsth o thr nd maoe hou n
whiteone viv itheof to sort wasdoz
lyatElysantlys t eevea might llyrines
        soPil - long?

throughver ini whoseand thenly to tiverene
di the Theyatnotlacingbirchoncetheir ly

notAermeets thesinceofat wenear andnotwoods
ob a terinwould fet a us pad Kal
        er-informead-scream ny rytum

me bor be

4


    heTPo e ns


ngt e ro st for p lneuh mnld, b rds erthnS
a ybin ouo rmthw b ay ngl o spe auia thgl
dl gr r rr ashfGre se ie rmndGs



              d - n sqrd ndCsmo
      fththth rbc rnk b t oewh ihhs


Aou ng eaae nde r                    t                        th    r du
a ttl r          f ware    o ll                    o t lde
                St    ostsii         s e l tho
  sth t i    r    b    estcw e        te        ee
                          e        rthr rH i  nd
                            dwh dpl e
                              tmdprl rt,
t hltht shh swh e atveth mf dn nd e aie
                      ean byo odo


                  a o esb lyho n
    tsles A hw ea t.  Th ant


                    th t?


  r e et ii om l h artess oung *s* rkttth
             r.  C lsthrssp er
  q *nernthk* d oera o dw o e n d nth nsw
          Jp w k; Wnd, t a *pstw* e ty


nw dph y wb ck e tcq tslyP. M. - T ckyc
     e sptd etw rc te Th heskoenpr
          ynst wl t rea h d b o
    k        a        ryl
        a     o n


    ly                    kn
    nc ea w d  s, ba        r
             m ut
      i
    ryn
gr e       e       l a s, h
i       k v  ooa e

# Wild Wilds

## Gary Snyder

(1930–)

[Dogen's] mountains and [rivers] are the processes of this earth, all of existence, process, essence, action, absence; they roll being and nonbeing together. They are what we are, we are what they are. For those who would see directly into essential nature, the idea of the sacred is a delusion and an obstruction: it diverts us from seeing what is before our eyes: plain thusness. . . . This, *thusness*, is the nature of the nature of nature. The wild in wild.

FOLLOWING JEFFERS AND REXROTH, GARY SNYDER IS the third great ecopoet of the California landscape, and this passage about Dogen's "Mountains and Rivers Sutra" summarizes his philosophical interests. Dogen (1200–1253) is the most influential of Japan's Zen masters and a prolific writer. His "mountains and rivers" is the Chinese (and later, Japanese) term relegated to "landscape" in translation, as in "landscape painting" or "landscape poetry," but in Snyder's description is indistinguishable from Tao (see p. 7), that ontological tissue in constant transformation. And Snyder's "thusness" is essentially *tzu-jan* (a concept that appears in Snyder's essays): Tao seen as the ten thousand individual things we encounter in *contact*. This mountains-and-rivers cosmology is central to his poetic thinking, thinking that drew primarily from non-Western sources, above all Ch'an (Zen) Buddhism.

At the same time that the middle-aged Cage was discovering Suzuki's Zen in New York City, a young Gary Snyder was discovering Zen in the wide-open high-alpine landscapes of the far West, where he began reading books on Zen by Suzuki and on haiku by R. H. Blythe. Eventually, he went to Japan and practiced for many years in monasteries: meditation and koan practice through which Zen opens students to their original empty minds, free of the conceptual structures of self-identity and social assumptions and the ongoing train of self-absorbed thought, thus returning them to that immediate experience of *contact* with the world as pure mystery, as "mountains and rivers" or Tao. Zen originated and evolved to maturity in China; so through his lifelong practice, ancient Chinese culture had a profound influence on him. But that influence was much broader, including especially Taoist thought, Ch'an's conceptual source, and classical Chinese poetry.

With its simple language of *tzu-jan*, the thusness of landscape and concrete image, classical Chinese poetry was the most defining poetic influence of Snyder's formative years. Mountains-and-rivers poetry is the heart of this tradition, and Snyder was engaged by a wide range of poets, studying them in the original as a graduate student. Snyder also wrote haiku, that extension of classical Chinese poetry. It was a kind of spiritual practice, for it focuses relentlessly on thusness as a Ch'an practice, and it was widely influential among poets at the time. Snyder actively exchanged haiku with his literary compatriots: Jack Kerouac, Allen Ginsberg, Philip Whalen, Lew Welch. Kerouac wrote large numbers of haiku, and indeed this interest in haiku extended as far as Richard Wright in his Paris exile, who was so intensely engaged with haiku practice during the last eighteen months of his life (1959–60) that he produced no less than four thousand of them.

Snyder himself was especially captivated by Cold Mountain (Han Shan), who was an ancient Chinese poet both of mountain landscape and Ch'an insight, all manifest in an abhorrence at convention and a wild delight in existence. In this, Cold Mountain was the perfect exemplar for Snyder, a kind of talisman, for Snyder's poetry as it developed might be described the same way. Cold Mountain lived on the fringes of a Ch'an monastic sangha at Cold Mountain sometime in the seventh to ninth centuries, and he so identified with the mountain that he took its name as his own (a practice typical of Ch'an masters). Indeed there are poems in which you can't tell them apart. And he was so wild that he only wrote his poems on rocks and trees (where the pine-ash ink would dissolve away in the next rainfall). That is how the legend describes Cold Mountain, and it goes on to say a local official collected those poems into a book that was preserved, lasting into the twentieth century, when Snyder reinvented Cold Mountain as a modern American poet in a group of very influential translations (p. 141).

In his cultivation of *tzu-jan* thusness, Snyder supplemented ancient Chinese culture with primitive cultures, an extension of Pound/Fenollosa's and Olson's interest in the primitive. He studied primitive cultures extensively as a student of anthropology, and in his essay "Poetry and the Primitive," he writes that in primitive societies

> people live vastly in the present. Their daily reality is a fabric of friends and family, the field of feeling and energy that one's own body is, the earth they stand on and the wind that wraps around it; and various areas of consciousness.

And further, that

> Of all the streams of civilized tradition with roots in the paleolithic, poetry is one of the few that can realistically claim an unchanged function and a relevance which will outlast most of the activities that surround us today. Poets, as few others, must live close to the world that primitive men are in: the world, in its nakedness, that is fundamental for all of us—birth, love, death; the sheer fact of being alive.

Primitive consciousness is consciousness prior to the evolution of the West's isolated "soul" or "spirit-center," prior to the alienating social constructions of Western civilization. It is consciousness in lifelong *contact* with the wild, a state in which the outer wilderness and inner wilderness are one and the same. Snyder is a very influential social figure, and the lack of *contact* with the wild was fundamental to his radical critique of Western civilization, as he describes in an essay entitled "The Wilderness":

> a culture that alienates itself from the very ground of its own being— from wilderness outside (that is to say, wild nature, the wild,

self-contained, self-informing ecosystems) and from that other wilderness, the wilderness within— is doomed to a very destructive behavior, ultimately perhaps self-destructive behavior.

Like his predecessors (Jeffers, Rexroth, Olson, Cage), Snyder saw that destructive behavior everywhere, the result of alienated white males struggling to dominate the world around them: environmental devastation, military aggression (especially America's genocidal campaign in Vietnam), racism, sexism, etc. Nature was devalued because it only exists to support "man." Women and dark-skinned people were at some level identified with the otherness of nature. Snyder is especially revered as an environmental activist, and he found the root source of the West's environmental devastation to be the dominant conceptual framework of Western civilization. It was described in a seminal and widely influential essay by Lynn White, "The Historical Roots of Our Ecological Crisis" (1967), which Snyder summarizes like this:

> Lynn White puts the blame for the present ecological crisis on the Judeo-Christian tradition—animals don't have souls and can't be saved; nature is merely a ground for us to exploit while working out our drama of free will and salvation under the watch of Jehovah.

For Snyder, the essence of self-cultivation is *contact*, the cultivation of *tzu-jan* thusness, and it is also an essential political imperative. Here Zen and the primitive meet, for Zen returns consciousness to the primitive, to consciousness prior to the evolution of self-identity and social assumptions and the intensely self-absorbed machinery of thought—all of which together separate us from immediate reality, consciousness in the immediate presence of *thusness*. And so, in both cases, it is a return to wilderness. When the mind is in *contact* it is returned to its wild state, free of the conditioning imposed by conventional society and politics and religion, and there it is integral to wilderness, wild mountains-and-rivers landscape.

These were not just a bundle of ideas for Snyder. He determined, not unlike Thoreau at Walden, to actually live them as a matter of immediate experience. The life he constructed became a kind of mythic ideal for the alternative culture, and his poetry is a very concrete and direct expression of that life. In addition to studying anthropology and East Asian cultures as a student, he famously spent two summers (1952–53) as a fire lookout on remote peaks in the Cascade Mountains (followed by Philip Whalen and Jack Kerouac, who wrote signature works there). Snyder made the high-altitude isolation into a kind of Buddhist practice; and he wrote his first mature poems there, poems heavily influenced by Chinese poetry (p. 142). After spending the better part of a decade practicing at Zen monasteries in Japan, Snyder married a Japanese woman at the lip of an active volcano on a barely inhabited Pacific island, whereupon he writes:

> It is possible at last for Masa and me to imagine a little of what the ancient—archaic—mind and life of Japan were. And to see what could be restored to the life today. A lot of it is
> simply in being aware of clouds and wind.

Eventually, they settled in the foothills of California's Sierra Nevada mountains, where they lived simply and raised a family as part of an alternative community of kindred spirits, cultivating a life of immediate *contact*, inhabiting "birth, love, death; the sheer fact of being alive" as part of the Sierra Nevada mountains and rivers in the full sense he found in Dogen's "Mountains and Rivers Sutra."

The sense of the Cosmos as living and ever-generative that infuses Dogen's mountains and rivers: it shapes both ancient Chinese and primitive cultures. And it is fundamental to Snyder, for whom *contact* is in the end a matter of *belonging* to that Cosmos. In this, his thought is manifestly deep-ecological, and his poetry manifestly ecopoetic. "Everything was alive—the trees, grasses, and winds were dancing with me, talking with me; I could understand the songs of the birds," he quotes an Arapaho dancer as saying. And he comments:

> This ancient experience is not so much—in spite of later commentators—"religious" as it is a pure perception of beauty. The phenomenal world experienced at certain pitches is totally living, exciting, mysterious, filling one with a trembling awe, leaving one grateful and humble. The wonder of the mystery returns direct to one's own senses and consciousness: inside and outside; the voice breathes, "Ah!"

This could as well be a description of Snyder's own poetry. With his language of gritty thusness, Snyder's poetic thought is made almost entirely of things (*tzu-jan*)—a singular reinvention of Pound's imagist poetics. And

moving with the primal energy of wildness (*wu-wei*), it brings Olson's po-
etics to fruition. It gives individual voice to the mystery of a universe that
is "a vast breathing body" (Tao), using that primitive breath-energy in all
the ways Olson describes to create something akin to an oral poetry at once
primitive and modern in its incantation of that ecstatic "Ah!"

## from COLD MOUNTAIN POEMS

### 6

Men ask the way to Cold Mountain
Cold Mountain: there's no through trail.
In summer, ice doesn't melt
The rising sun blurs in swirling fog.
How did I make it?
My heart's not the same as yours.
If your heart was like mine
You'd get it and be right here.

### 7

I settled at Cold Mountain long ago,
Already it seems like years and years.
Freely drifting, I prowl the woods and streams
And linger watching things themselves.
Men don't get this far into the mountains,
White clouds gather and billow.
Thin grass does for a mattress,
The blue sky makes a good quilt.
Happy with a stone underhead
Let heaven and earth go about their changes.

# MID-AUGUST AT SOURDOUGH MOUNTAIN LOOKOUT

Down valley a smoke haze
Three days heat, after five days rain
Pitch glows on the fir-cones
Across rocks and meadows
Swarms of new flies.

I cannot remember things I once read
A few friends, but they are in cities.
Drinking cold snow-water from a tin cup
Looking down for miles
Through high still air.

## BURNING THE SMALL DEAD

Burning the small dead
      branches
broke from beneath
  thick spreading
        whitebark pine.

      a hundred summers
snowmelt     rock    and  air

hiss in a twisted bough.

  sierra granite;
       Mt. Ritter—
       black rock twice as old.

Deneb, Altair

windy fire

# WAVE

Grooving clam shell
        streakt through marble,
     sweeping down ponderosa pine bark-scale
       rip-cut tree grain
           sand-dunes, lava
           flow

Wave        wife.
        woman — wyfman —
"veiled;   vibrating;   vague"
  sawtooth ranges pulsing;
            veins on the back of the hand.

Forkt out: birdsfoot-alluvium
        wash

     great dunes rolling
Each inch rippld, every grain a wave.

Leaning against sand cornices til they blow away

  —wind, shake
  stiff thorns of cholla, ocotillo
  sometimes I get stuck in thickets—

Ah, trembling spreading radiating wyf
        racing zebra
  catch me and fling me wide
To the dancing grain of things
         of my mind!

# ANASAZI

Anasazi,
Anasazi,

tucked up in clefts in the cliffs
growing strict fields of corn and beans
sinking deeper and deeper in earth
up to your hips in Gods
          you head all turned to eagle-down
          & lightning for knees and elbows
your eyes full of pollen

          the smell of bats.
          the flavor of sandstone
          grit on the tongue.

          women
          birthing
at the foot of ladders in the dark.

trickling streams in hidden canyons
under the cold rolling desert

corn-basket        wide-eyed
          red baby
          rock lip home,

Anasazi

## THE WAY WEST, UNDERGROUND

The split-cedar
smoked salmon
cloudy days of Oregon,
the thick fir forests.

       Black Bear heads uphill in
       Plumas county,
       round bottom scuttling through willows—

The Bear Wife moves up the coast.

       where blackberry brambles
       ramble in the burns.

And around the curve of islands
foggy volcanoes
on, to North Japan. The bears
& fish-spears of the Ainu.
Gilyak.
Mushroom-vision healer,
single flat drum,
from long before China.

Women with drums who fly over Tibet.

Following forests west, and
rolling, following grassland,
tracking bears and mushrooms,
eating berries all the way.
In Finland finally took a bath:
       like redwood sweatlodge on the Klamath—
all the Finns in moccasins and
pointy hats with dots of white,

netting, trapping, bathing,
singing holding hands, the while

see-sawing on a bench, a look of love—

Karhu—Bjorn—Braun—Bear

      [lightning rainbow great cloud tree
              dialogs of birds]
Europa.    'The West.'
the bears are gone
              except Brunhilde?

Or elder wilder goddesses reborn—will race
   the streets of France and Spain
         with automatic guns—
        in Spain,
Bears and Bison,
Red Hands with missing fingers,
red mushroom labyrinths;
lightning-bolt mazes,
painted in caves,

underground.

# THE BATH

Washing Kai in the sauna,
The kerosene lantern set on a box
    outside the ground-level window,
Lights up the edge of the iron stove and the
    washtub down on the slab
Steaming air and crackle of waterdrops
    brushed by on the pile of rocks on top
He stands in warm water
Soap all over the smooth of his thigh and stomach
    "Gary don't soap my hair!"
    —his eye-sting fear—
    the soapy hand feeling
    through and around the gloves and curves of his body
    up in the crotch,
And washing-tickling out the scrotum, little anus,
    his penis curving up and getting hard
    as I pull back skin and try to wash it
Laughing and jumping, flinging arms around,
    I squat all naked too,
                      *is this our body?*

Sweating and panting in the stove-steam hot-stone
    cedar-planking wooden bucket water-splashing
    kerosene lantern-flicker wind-in-the-pines-out
    sierra forest ridges night—
Masa comes in, letting fresh cool air
    sweep down from the door
    a deep sweet breath
And she tips him over gripping neatly, one knee down
    her hair falling hiding one whole side of
    shoulder, breast, and belly,
Washes deftly Kai's head-hair
    as he gets mad and yells—
The body of my lady, the winding valley spine,

the space between the thighs I reach through,
  cup her curving vulva arch and hold if from behind,
  a soapy tickle          a hand of grail
The gates of Awe
That open back a turning double-mirror world of
  wombs in wombs, in rings,
  that start in music,
                    *is this our body?*

The hidden place of seed
The veins net flow across the ribs, that gathers
  milk and peaks up in a nipple—fits
  our mouth—
The sucking milk from this our body sends through
  jolts of light; the son, the father,
  sharing mother's joy
That brings a softness to the flower of the awesome
  open curling lotus gate I cup and kiss
As Kai laughs at his mother's breast he now is weaned
  from, we
  wash each other,
                    *this our body*

Kai's little scrotum up close to his groin,
  the seed still tucked away, that moved from us to him
In flows that lifted with the same joys forces
  as his nursing Masa later,
  playing with her breast,
Or me within her,
Or him emerging,
                    *this is our body:*

Clean, and rinsed, and sweating more, we stretch
  out on the redwood benches hearts all beating
Quiet to the simmer of the stove,
  the scent of cedar
And then turn over,

      murmuring gossip of the grasses,
      talking firewood,
Wondering how Gen's napping, how to bring him in
      soon wash him too—
These boys who love their mother
      who loves men, who passes on
      her sons to other women;

The cloud across the sky. The windy pines.
      the trickle gurgle in the swampy meadow

    *this is our body.*

Fire inside and boiling water on the stove
We sigh and slide ourselves down from the benches
      wrap the babies, step outside,

black night & all the stars.

Pour cold water on the back and thighs
Go in the house—stand steaming by the center fire
Kai scampers on the sheepskin
Gen standing hanging on and shouting,

"Bao! bao! bao! bao! bao!"

This is our body. Drawn up crosslegged by the flames
      drinking icy water
      hugging babies, kissing bellies,

Laughing on the Great Earth

Come out from the bath.

# PRAYER FOR THE GREAT FAMILY

Gratitude to Mother Earth, sailing through night and day—
    and to her soil: rich, rare, and sweet
        *in our minds so be it.*

Gratitude to Plants, the sun-facing light-changing leaf
    and fine root-hairs; standing still through wind
    and rain; their dance is in the flowing spiral grain
        *in our minds so be it.*

Gratitude to Air, bearing the soaring Swift and the silent
    Owl at dawn. Breath of our song
    clear spirit breeze
        *in our minds so be it.*

Gratitude to Wild Beings, our brothers and sisters, teaching
    secrets, freedoms, and ways; who share with us their
    milk; self-complete, brave, and aware
        *in our minds so be it.*

Gratitude to Water: clouds, lakes, rivers, glaciers;
    holding or releasing; streaming through all
    our bodies salty seas
        *in our minds so be it.*

Gratitude to the Sun: blinding pulsing light through
    trunks of trees, through mists, warming caves where
    bears and snakes sleep—he who wakes us—
        *in our minds so be it.*

Gratitude to the Great Sky
    who holds billions of stars—and goes yet beyond that—
    beyond all powers, and thoughts

and yet is within us—
Grandfather Space.
The Mind is his Wife.

*so be it.*

*after a Mohawk prayer*

# O WATERS

      O waters
    wash us, me,
under the wrinkled granite
     straight-up slab,

and sitting by camp in the pine shade
Nanao sleeping,
mountains humming and crumbling
      snowfields melting
      soil
      building on tiny ledges
for wild onions and the flowers
        Blue
    Polemonium

      great
      earth
      sangha

# RAVEN'S BEAK RIVER AT THE END

Doab of the Tatshenshini River and the Alsek Lake, a long spit of gravel,
one clear day after days on the river in the rain, the glowing sandy slopes
of Castilleja blooms & little fox tracks in the moose-print swales, & giant
scoops of dirt took out by bears around the lupine roots, at early light a rim
of snowy mountains and the ice fields slanting back for miles, I find my way

>To the boulders
>>on the gravel    in the flowers
>At the end of the glacier
>>two ravens
>Sitting on a boulder
>>carried by the glacier
>Left on the gravel
>>resting in the flowers
>At the end of the ice age
>>show me the way
>To a place to sit
>>in a hollow on a boulder
>Looking east, looking south
>>ear in the river
>Running just behind me
>>nose in the grasses
>Vetch roots scooped out
>>by the bears in the gravels
>Looking up the ice slopes
>>ice plains, rock-fall
>Brush-line, dirt-sweeps
>>on the ancient river
>Blue queen floating in
>>ice lake, ice throne, end of a glacier
>Looking north
>>up the dancing river
>Where it turns into a glacier
>>under stairsteps of ice falls

Green streaks of alder
    climb the mountain knuckles
Interlaced with snowfields
    foamy water falling
Salmon weaving river
    bear flower    blue sky singer
As the raven leaves her boulder
    flying over flowers
Raven-sitting high spot
    eyes on the snowpeaks,
Nose of morning
    raindrops in the sunshine
Skin of sunlight
    skin of chilly gravel
Mind in the mountains, mind of tumbling water,
    mind running rivers,
Mind of sifting
    flowers in the gravels
At the end of the ice age
    we are the bears, we are the ravens,
We are the salmon
    in the gravel
At the end of an ice age
Growing on the gravels
    at the end of a glacier
Flying off alone
    flying off alone
    flying off alone


Off alone

# Mammal Wilds

## *Michael McClure*

(1932–)

MICHAEL McCLURE IS ANOTHER WEST COAST POET engaged in reimagining the question of *who we are* in relation to *where we are*. McClure takes the most fundamental issue to be the socially and politically constructed identity imposed on individuals, making them into useful "products" serving a system of economic and military despoliation. This compounds the more traditional assumption that consciousness is a rational "soul" ontologically different from and alien to the physical body, which the puritanical society of the time suppressed in destructive ways. For McClure, as for his predecessors, this soul-product in its repressed alienation from body and earth was responsible for war, environmental destruction, and the alienation of individuals from their deepest potentialities for joy and wholeness and self-realization as physical beings. And so, his poetic practice is an act of political rebellion (he was also politically active in the more conventional sense in antiwar and environmental campaigns) against a culture where people had "so little interior and individuated self remaining."

In opposition to society's assumptions, McClure the deep ecologist proposes that we stop thinking of ourselves as souls, even as human, and start thinking of ourselves as mammal, as integral to the tissue of an organic and living and generative Cosmos. The understanding that we are in fact mammal and primate was hardly new as a scientific proposition, but it had not at all begun to be felt at the level of consciousness and immediate experience. And once felt at that level, this understanding opens an experience of the Cosmos that combines modern scientific understanding with Taoist insights from ancient China:

> What I'm speaking of is the Taoist notion that the universe that we perceive is an "uncarved block," that all time/space occurrences of the past, present, and future are one giant sculpture of which we're a part. It's not as if something is going to exist in the future or that something has happened in the past, but that it's all going on at once. And we're in it. If we're aware of that, there's a *proportionlessness* that is a liberating state or condition.

Lao Tzu speaks of this uncarved block a number of times, identifying it with Tao, as in this passage: "Tao is perennially nameless, / an uncarved simplicity." That is, *Tao* describes physical reality as a single generative tissue that shapes itself into the ten thousand things, which are reality as we know it through immediate perception. McClure returns to the concept again, recognizing that this Taoist Cosmos entails a by now familiar sense of time, not as linear but as an ongoing generative moment: "The organism is a swirl of environment in what the Taoists call the Uncarved Block of time and space (a universe in which time and space are not separated into intersecting facets . . .)."

Dramatically announcing his ecopoetic intent, McClure attempts to create this whole galactic-mammal experience through wild typography and language, all deployed through Olson's breath-energy of the body. But remarkably, in the midst of the primal roar of his poetry, there is a current of gentleness and vulnerability and even humor, a dimension informed by his longtime practice of Ch'an. His poems are best experienced when read aloud, as oral poetry, and take an early and particularly radical form in his *Ghost Tantras* (pp. 160-63), which are written largely in meaningless "beast language." Quite different in intent from Cage's meaningless texts, McClure's poems carry us past the human meaning-making of language (medium of that rational soul as "product") to a more primal mammal level of expression. And indeed, the title referring to Tantric Buddhism suggests a sexual dimension often heard in the sounds, for sex is perhaps a modern person's most powerful connection to the primitive. Physiologically, when read aloud *Ghost Tantras* open the tight breath-control that makes spoken language—and so, physically liberate us into our more primal body-selves. Interestingly, this beast language is sometimes mixed with conventional language, implying that our conventional language is in fact "beast language." And this is McClure's point: under the veneer of respectability that enables everyday life in the economic/military order, a veneer embodied in the workaday utilitarian language that dominates our mental processes, lies our more real mammal selves.

To reinvent thought/identity at a fundamental level means reinventing language. McClure's poems, with their cascades of language and idea and image, are meant to induce a revelation experience in which we feel ourselves at this primal level of existence as mammal, as a swirl in the galactic onslaught of interpenetration and transformation. Poetry is traditionally considered a cerebral activity of the intellect/soul, but McClure remakes it into an animal gesture: spontaneous and wild. He thought of the poem as a physical and living extension of his animal nature, an idea that undermines the traditional assumption that language is a kind of spirit realm altogether separate from the physical (like the soul), a realm that mimetically represents the physical. Hence, a rewilding of language, the medium of thought, as part of the galactic swirl of earth-energy.

In the end, this is a poetry of radical *contact* in which, free of the isolated self/soul, "our experience of the universe is also the universe perceiving itself." McClure distills this whole project of mammalian transcendence here in this preface to one of his long poems:

> I am one with the euglena, triceratops, mammoth and sea urchin. I am one with the universe of matter and energy as well as the fields that I do not know of consciously or verbally. All these are contained within myself. My self, or selves, is a part of all. The surge may be inter-universal—may drift through all time and space. I am an extrusion, a tentacle, a point, a pip, upon or within this happening.
>
> Yet I am no more or less important than the whole. Politics and social strata are a natural projection (among many possible projections) of my closest of all cousins. They tell me that I am a man. I know that I am a mammal and part of ALL. I want cousinship and I write rapidly and without judgment to make an artifact that is less and less a part of the social strata of Man. I wish to make a poem that is an act of nature—more free of the conditioning that I call politics.

# GHOST TANTRAS

## 15 b

HRAHH ! GRAHHR ! WRAH ! GROOOOOOOOOOO !
BEEEEYAIRE MWAHH HRR-R-R-R-R-R
Frooooo mwahh tooogartooniee hrrrrrr noooor
by you come back here me nye too thoh !
SHRAHH ! SHRAHH !
WEERBNOOOR, HUHFWOOOO, HREHHHH,
oh I miss you, love, you here with bree reth
*gahnoor* bye weeb-doo lagg brekk-artnotty,
BWOOOOO,
WEEB TERR,
but me hool voo narg narr.

YAHRHOOON NAHGROOOR OON MEEELT !
OOHN ESS TATH HAR FREEDOM.
GRAHHR ! GAHOOOOOOR GRAHH-GAHR !
The heavy curtains are raised
by roaring
upward flowing with implesharr grahh grace.
Blackness upon white and heavenly coloring
frahhn gahr groooh gahoor rahhr ! Grah !
Hrahhr thah noose eeelt em tell.
DROOOOOOSHOOOON ! SHHROO-
OOOOO !
Fine green ferns amidst crevices
and wet trailing moss upon logs in streams !
Thah hoors ess freee.

## 98

GRAHH HARR GAHHR HRAHH GOOOOOORHH !
GARHH GAHHHRRRR ! GAHROOOOH, AYE !
GAHHR GAHRHOOO-RHEER GRAHAHH ! OH
thah neert gahhr grahgmn grhh drt gahr grayhayoar
nyarr grooh hrahh grahrgmn grooor HAHHR !
GRAHIEE THOW VAROOM SENTIENT GAHRGRR
JOINER OF TIME, SPACE & GAHREEEOH
GAHHR-HOOOM NEORR GAHRRGRAGM HRAHRR.
AY HI MEOH GARGM GRAHHRR GAHOOOOO
THEEER GRAHDOON HROHH NYORR !
Gahr ghrmayorhrrr. Grayhoww no ooobleosh.
GAHHHHHR !
SEEEZMEOH-SHORNETT
GROOOOOOOOOOOOOOOH ! GAHRRR !

99

IN TRANQUILITY THY GRAHRR AYOHH
ROOHOOERING
GRAHAYAOR GAHARRR GRAHHR GAHHR
THEOWSH NARR GAHROOOOOOOOH GAHRR
GRAH GAHRRR ! GRAYHEEOARR GRAHRGM
THAHRR NEEOWSH DYE YEOR GAHRR
grah grooom gahhr nowrt thowtooom obleeomosh.
AHH THEEAHH ! GAHR GRAH NAYEEROOOO
GAHROOOOOM GRHH GARAHHRR OH THY
NOOOSHEORRTOMESH GREEEEGRAHARRR
OH THOU HERE, HERE, HERE IN MY FLESH
RAISING THE CURTAIN
HAIEAYORR-REEEEHORRRR
in tranquility.

# THE SKULL

*for Charles Olson and Jack Kerouac*

WE SHALL BE SWIRLS — SWIRLS — SWIRLS
OF EXPANDING STRUCTURE
and make our New Pleistocene
among the STARS!
WE SHALL BE MEN ((MAMMALS!!))
of infinite beauty!
THE SURGE
will
pour
UNSTOPPABLE.

We shall arise like jeweled
CROWNS
from a hurled stone
in a still pool.

ALL
begins
with OUR protein!
WE ARE THE SUN! WE ARE THE SURFACE
SPREADING,
retopologizing,
SPORING . . .

WE SHALL GROWL — AND WE SHALL SING!!

# THE SKULL

## ROLLS & COILS AS THE CREATURE

# MAN-MAMMAL

## UPSTANDS

PARIETAL SWELLS TO FRONT AND BACK
(Occiput accommodates the vision. Dark holes of seeing.)

CORTEX FLOWS BOTH BACKWARD AND UPWARD
TO FIND THE BALANCE

ABOVE PELVIS — HEART — LUNG AND GUT.

The constellative complexities of sensorium

SWELL IN A MULTITUDINOUS MIME
OF BEING—SCANNED
BY A SOURCE THAT IS CENTRAL
ONLY TO THE POLYTHEISM

OF SELF

self

*SELF*
*(Selves)*          SELF          *SELF*
                                  *(Selves)*

self

SELF

SELVES MAKING A CONGRESS
OF MEAT-NOTHING

NO SELF LESS URGENT THAN ANOTHER
IN THE CONGRESS.

THE CHAMBERS OF THE EAR ARE THERE
FOR THE SNOW LEOPARD, THE WOLF,
the lichen, and the salmon to speak to.


HE RAISES HIMSELF AND THE BONE
CHAMBER (HOME
OF BEINGS EQUAL TO HEART AND TO GLAND)
WOBBLES AND BALANCES . . .
TURNS SEARCHING
FOR FOOD, WARMTH, FRONTIER, SEX, LOVE . . .

is powered
BY THE BULK OF THE MEAT THAT IS
MAMMAL REAL MEMORY AND WEIGHT
AND SOURCE
DERIVED FROM THE INERT SURFACE
ENERGIED BY SUN . . . ENERGIED
BY QUINTILLIONIC GENERATIONS
OF SUN GALAXIES
in past and present future
OF NOW . . .


—IS forever brilliant and unforgetting . . .
knows six billion years of the sculpture
of living surging (ONE CREATURE) plasm
that dances like a sculpture freed
of
TIME                                        SPACE,
NO
MORE
or less
meaningless or meaningful
THAN A MOLECULE OR BACTERIUM

OR
any facet,
extrusion, or aura
OF THE MEAT

bone   claw   tentacle   fur   tooth   scale   feather
stamen   spore


in the swirl-whirling systemless-system, extending
and containing through ellipsis the perceptions and insights
INTO THE IMAGINED INVISIBLE

in which star systems are likewise

PROPORTIONLESS PARTICLES

# WHERE

THE BLACK RIVER
becoming Ocean

BREATHE-BEATS
(groomed by seals and sea birds)

## IS

sailed by ships and seed fluff
of imaginary physical-molecular
IMAGINATION . . .

does not                    dream
BUT KNOWS
in many ways
the laugh, the joy, the screams

OF DRAGONS
dragoning themselves

AND FINDS THE CONFLUENCES THAT BURST

OUT AND JOIN

AGAIN . . . DEVOURS

BECOMES    COUSINS

with all creatures,
jasper, jade, lapis, cellulose, phosphorous,
crystals, fluids. —SYSTEMS INCONCEIVABLE
even to this open system
TOUCH     &     BRUSH
the thorns, velvet, musk,


DIVIDE,
EXTRUDE FROM THE BULK,


REGARD


SELF
(selves)
as tool!
REJECT!   REJECT!
Finds confluence
then
confluence of confluence of confluence . . .
CREATES SHIP OR THISTLEDOWN WITH IMAGE
(condor, atom, galaxy, wolf, cobra, raptor)
on the sails.


SETS OUT


AS (skull) CONFLUENCES (skull) MERGE (skull)


sailing


BA, KA, CHI, PRANA, MEAT, SPIRIT, ODEM.


UPSTANDS    FROM    THE    PRONE    LIMBS
(arm)         (leg)      (toe)      (penis)      (digit)

ALL WAYS
(freed from the instant experience).

Horseback in Libya with Bow. Hunting Old Stone Age by
new star
(covered with fur or not).


PROPORTIONLESS          MELTED
of predisposition
destroyed
(recreated),


MYTHOLOGIES MADE
(instant by instant)
living, sightful, worm-writhing,
THE OLD BRAIN
(in biologic precedence)
balanced against
VISION

VISIONLESS
(as!                    !one)

SYMBOL-LESS.
The symbol being

A BLACK DOT

encircled by a band of Halo

Held aloft by wings of falcon.
(*pinions*)              (*pinions*)
A dark drop

falls from
the flying globe.
TWO DROPS SPRAY
from the sphere.

Two drops spurt from each drop.
EACH
glistens with radiance.

Smoke spurts from the North of the Globe.


IT IS MIRRORED.

It repeats

finitely      infinitely

# GATHERING DRIFTWOOD ON
# CHRISTMAS MORNING

OLD APPLES FROM DARK SWANS
DROP IN MY HEART.
NO!
Not "Heart"
but
SOUL
—or say "Spirit"
as spirit is glassy peaks
of living foam reflecting waves
upon wet sand on Christmas Day.
From above stare down steep hills with veins
of serpentine and chaparral slowly roaring
toward the sea.
And we are ONE and ALL—held together
by
this fantasy
of sun and grin and meatly
molecules.
And it riffles slightly at the edges
like a calm but smirking
almost merry dream.

# A LITTLE TIBETAN POEM

EGO OBSESSIONS DRY UP THE BRAIN
TO SCULPTURES
of
revenge-acts
and then reverberate
(to tear the beautiful arms
to aching bones).
I
SAY
I
AM
A
LOVELY
LOVELY
LOVELY
MOUNTAIN
IN THE RAIN
with cool waterfalls
and scents of fir trees
round my ears.
I laugh high above the plain.
Little clouds are drifting by my nose.

DEER BONES AND FOX SCATS
dry in the late
spring sun
watched over
by
yellow mule-ears
and blue-eyed grass.

| | |
|---|---|
| Buckwheat | Cries |
| Brodiaea | of hummingbirds |
| Bunch grass | in |
| A vulture (close) | the |
| Bee plant | wind |
| Crab spider | on |
| Garter snake | the path |
| Seaside daisy | through |
| Grindelia | the chaparral. |
| Coyote bush | Bright |
| Poison oak | vision |
| Cow parsnip | light. |
| Wild iris | Ocean |
| Baeria | below. |
| Buttercup | Hello, |
| | Lew! |

*Note*: Lew Welch was another prominent poet in the Snyder/McClure circle of Beat poets. He vanished into the woods with a rifle and apparently shot himself not long before McClure wrote this poem.

# PUCK

THE SERIOUSNESS OF ANIMALS
IS
MONUMENTAL!
The absolute intention of the snake fly
and the bee and the tiny creatures
that zoom in the sun
among pine boughs. And the arthropods
mating! Even the play of the rats
and the rabbits is serious.
What a perfect world!
Without entry or escape!
EVEN
where the

MEAT-WE

splits
into two
branches—even though
we look across at insects
from a fork
a billion years
cleft away
in evolution
IT

IS

ALL

THIS

SERIOUS

WORLD

—and to be carefree
is to be a soft and laughing star.

## UNCHANGED

NO MEAT, NO MIND, NO CONSCIOUSNESS,
NO ONE TO BE FREE OF DARKNESS
OR FOR THE LIGHT TO FIND IN UNIVERSES OF WHITE EAGLE
WINGS—WHERE I HAVE BEEN WITH YOU!
With no regret we will leave
as if we
WERE NEVER HERE
holding it precious and perfect
IN THE ONGOING NOTHINGNESS
((^ ^ ^ ^
^ ^ ^ ^ ^ ^ ^ ^ ^ ^))
BORN AND UNBORN, TASTES OF DARK CHOCOLATE,
touch of lavender cashmere,
NOT EVEN KNOWING
there's nothing
to
forget
—even tired arm muscles after swimming.
THIS IS OUR PERFECTION

# Primal Wilds

## *Jerome Rothenberg*

(*1931–*)

J EROME ROTHENBERG BECAME THE EPICENTER OF
that seismic impact the primitive had on post–World War II
poetry. His work was, not surprisingly, itself a vortex of wild energy: an
onslaught of anthologies, poems, translations, essays, manifestos, perfor-
mances. He led an amorphous movement beginning in the late 1950s and
early '60s that he called "ethnopoetics." The ethnopoetics project cen-
ters on a revaluing of the primitive—as in Rothenberg's axiom "primitive
means complex"—with an ultimate interest in confirming and encourag-
ing the opening of innovative poetry and consciousness, proposing poetry
as a new "totality" that includes all of the "old excluded orders": the primi-
tive, female, foreign, earth, animal and vegetal, body, sexual, unconscious,
unknown, etc. Hence, ethnopoetics as "a complex redefinition of cultural
and intellectual values."

Rothenberg's insights into the primitive were reinforced by several years
living with the Seneca Indians, and those insights led logically to a singular
working method that embodied those values of inclusion and otherness.
For him, ethnopoetics was a kind of framework that contained the voices
of many fellow travelers (including a number of the people presented in
this book: Pound/Fenollosa, Olson, Snyder, McClure, Merwin), collected
most notably in his *Symposium of the Whole: A Range of Discourse Toward
an Ethnopoetics*. And this working method shaped two widely influential

anthologies that collected primal poetry from throughout the world, *Technicians of the Sacred* (1968) and *Shaking the Pumpkin* (1972), as well as his magazine *Alcheringa: A Journal in Ethnopoetics* (1970–80). (To gauge the zeitgeist, it's worth noting that Rothenberg's anthologies were preceded in 1967 by another monumental collection of primitive poetry from around the world: Williard Trask's two-volume *The Unwritten Song*.)

Rothenberg thought of his anthologies "not so much as anthologies but as assemblages or collages," and more: "as (1) a manifesto; (2) a way of laying out an active poetics—by example and by commentary; and (3) a grand assemblage: a kind of art form in its own right." He thought of this work expressly as a way of deepening and expanding the possibilities for modern poetry; and even if some might say he romanticized the primitive, what matters for us is the ideas themselves and how they transform poetic thinking, offering in the "Pre-Face" to *Technicians* a list of intersections between radical modern poetry and the primal poetry he was collecting in his anthologies:

(1) the poem carried by the voice: a "pre"-literate situation of poetry . . .
(2) a highly developed process of image-thinking: concrete or non-causal thought . . .
(3) a "minimal" art of maximal involvement; compound elements, each clearly articulated, & with plenty of room for fill-in (gaps in sequence, etc.) . . .
(4) an "intermedia" situation, as further denial of the categories: the poet's techniques aren't limited to verbal maneuvers but operate also through song, non-verbal sound, visual signs, & the varied activities of the ritual event . . .
(5) the animal-body-rootedness of "primitive" poetry . . .
(6) the poet as shaman . . . an open "visionary" situation prior to all system-making. . . .

The selection of poems below is drawn from Rothenberg's *Technicians of the Sacred* and *Shaking the Pumpkin*. Following the focus of this book, the selection draws only on work from North America. And meanwhile, as this book shares in some ways Rothenberg's methodology, it seems apt to construct a more detailed description of his ethnopoetic project as a collage of his own statements:

... the Senecas with whom I lived call ... themselves *"real* people" ... descended from a single mother (ultimately the Earth) . . . .

A "real" person in these terms is one who hasn't forgotten what & where things are in relation to the Earth. . . . He has only to maintain a true eye for his surroundings & a contact [Thoreau's word again!] with the Earth, to recognize himself as the inheritor of reality, of a more real way of life. . . .

The *real* person (reality-person, in fact) lives, like the "primitive" philosopher described by Radin, "in a blaze of reality" through which he can experience "reality at white heat." This is a part of the tribal inheritance (not Indian only but worldwide) that we all lose at our peril — younger and older alike. Remember too how many elements are active in that situation, where we would concentrate on the words as being particularly the "poem" (many Indian poems in fact dispense entirely with words): elements, I mean, like music, non-verbal phonetic sounds, dance, gesture & event, game, dream, etc., along with all those unstated ideas & images the participants pick up from the poem's context. Each moment is charged: each is a point at which meaning is coming to surface, where nothing's incidental but everything matters terribly.

Now, put all of that together & you have the makings of a high poetry & art, which only a colonialist ideology could have blinded us into labeling "primitive" or "savage." You have also the great hidden accomplishment of our older brothers in America, made clear in the poetry & yet of concern not only to poets but to all (red, white & black) who want to carry the possibilities of reality & personhood into any new worlds to come. . . . We're doomed without this tribal and matrilocal wisdom, which can be shared only among equals who have recognized a common lineage from the earth.

-------

... the most experimental and future-directed side of Romantic and modern poetry . . . has been the most significantly connected with the attempt to define an ethnopoetics.

There is a politics in all of this, and an importance, clearly, beyond the work of poets and artists. The old "primitive" models in particular — of small and integrated stateless and classless societies — reflect a concern over the last two centuries with new communalistic and anti-authoritarian forms of social life and with alternatives to the environmental disasters accompanying an increasingly abstract relation to what was once a living universe. Our belief in this regard is that a re-viewing of "primitive" ideas of the "sacred" represents an attempt—by poets and others—to preserve and enhance primary human values against a mindless mechanization that has run past any uses it may once have had . . . .

Few poets and artists—post–World War II—weren't somehow involved in these new mappings, for what had changed was our paradigm of what poetry was or now could come to be.

. . . to heal the break between reality and language. Something like this has been a central project of our work as poets—a key both to our search for a primal poetics and to our search for the sacred.

The sacred rather than the transcendent, because the transcendent . . . implies for me too great a denial of the here and now; and the source of poetry, as I understand it, is deeply rooted in the world around us: doesn't deny it so much as brings it back to life.

This search [for the primitive] . . . is felt as well, say, in the words of ancient Heraclitus often cited by Charles Olson: "Man is estranged from that with which he is most familiar."

Pound's writing, then, came at a moment in history when a debased poetry, an unanchored language of transcendence, had separated us from the immediacies of our experience (debilitating as that experience may have been) and when a new sacralization (the renewal of the spiritual-in-art) depended on connecting to the concrete particulars of the world around us.

What that [primitive] poetry transmits is not so much a sense of reverence or piety as of mystery & wonder.

. . . my work focused on *origins*—trans-human origins . . .

# MAGIC WORDS (AFTER NALUNGIAQ)

*Eskimo (Inuit)*

In the very earliest time,
when both people and animals lived on earth,
a person could become an animal if he wanted to
and an animal could become a human being.
Sometimes they were people
and sometimes animals
and there was no difference.
All spoke the same language.
That was the time when words were like magic.
The human mind had mysterious powers.
A word spoken by chance
might have strange consequences.
It would suddenly come alive
and what people wanted to happen could happen—
all you had to do was say it.
Nobody could explain this:
That's the way it was.

*English version by Edward Field, after Rasmussen*

# BEFORE THEY MADE THINGS BE ALIVE THEY SPOKE

*by Lucario Cuevish*

*Luiseño*

Earth woman lying flat her feet were to the north her head was to the south
Sky brother sitting on her right hand side he said Yes sister you must tell me
who you are She answered I am Tomaiyowit She asked him Who are you?
He answered I am Tukmit. Then she said:

> I stretch out flat to the Horizon.
> I shake I make a noise like thunder.
> I am Earthquake.
> I am round & roll around.
> I vanish & return.

Then Tukmit said:

> I arch above you like a lid.
> I deck you like a hat.
> I go up high & higher.
> I am death I gulp it in one bite.
> I grab men from the east & scatter them.
> My name is Death.

Then they made things be alive.

*English version by Jerome Rothenberg,*
*after Constance G. DuBois, after Preuss*

# THE EAGLE ABOVE US

*Cora*


he lives in the sky
far above us
the eagle
looks good there
has a good grip on his world

his world wrapt in grey
but a living a humid
a beautiful grey

there he glides in the sky
very far
right above us

waits for what Tetewan
netherworld goddess
has to say

bright
his eye
on his world

bright
his eye
on the water of life
the sea
embracing
the earth

frightful his face
radiant his eye
the sun

his feet a deep red
there he is
right above us

spreading his wings
he remembers
who dwell down below

among whom the gods
let rain fall let dew fall
for life on their earth

there above us he speaks
we can hear him
his words make great sound

deep down they go
where mother Tetewan hears him and answers
we can hear her

here they meet
her words and the eagle's
we hear them together
together they make great sound

eagle words
fading
far above the water of life

mother words
from deep down
sighing away through the vaults of the sky

*English version by Anselm Hollo*

*from* THE NIGHT CHANT
(*after Bitahatini*)

*Navajo*

In Tsegihi
In the house made of the dawn
In the house made of evening twilight
In the house made of dark cloud
In the house made of rain & mist, of pollen, of grasshoppers
Where the dark mist curtains the doorway
The path to which is on the rainbow
Where the zigzag lightning stands high on top
Where the he-rain stands high on top

O male divinity
With your moccasins of dark cloud, come to us
With your mind enveloped in dark cloud, come to us
With the dark thunder above you, come to us soaring
With the shapen cloud at your feet, come to us soaring
With the far darkness made of the dark cloud over your head, come to us soaring
With the far darkness made of the rain & mist over your head, come to us soaring
With the zigzag lightning flung out high over your head
With the rainbow hanging high over your head, come to us soaring
With the far darkness made of the rain & the mist on the ends of your wings,
     come to us soaring
With the far darkness of the dark cloud on the ends of your wings, come to
     us soaring
With the zigzag lightning, with the rainbow high on the ends of your wings,
     come to us soaring
With the near darkness made of the dark cloud of the rain & the mist,
     come to us
With the darkness on the earth, come to us

With these I wish the foam floating on the flowing water over the roots of the
     great corn
I have made your sacrifice

I have prepared a smoke for you
My feet restore for me
My limbs restore, my body restore, my mind restore, my voice restore for me
Today, take out your spell for me

Today, take away your spell for me
Away from me you have taken it
Far off from me it is taken
Far off you have done it

Happily I recover
Happily I become cool

My eyes regain their power, my head cools, my limbs regain their strength,
    I hear again

Happily the spell is taken off for me
Happily I walk, impervious to pain I walk, light within I walk, joyous I walk

Abundant dark clouds I desire
An abundance of vegetation I desire
An abundance of pollen, abundant dew, I desire

Happily may fair white corn come with you to the ends of the earth
Happily may fair yellow corn, fair blue corn, fair corn of all kinds, plants
    of all kinds, goods of all kinds, jewels of all kinds, come with you to
    the ends of the earth

With these before you, happily may they come with you
With these behind, below, above, around you, happily may they come with you
Thus you accomplish your tasks

Happily the old men will regard you
Happily the old women will regard you
The young men & the young women will regard you
The children will regard you
The chiefs will regard you

Happily as they scatter in different directions they will regard you
Happily as they approach their homes they will regard you

May their roads home be on the trail of peace
Happily may they all return

In beauty I walk
With beauty before me I walk
With beauty behind me I walk
With beauty above me I walk
With beauty above & about me I walk
It is finished in beauty
It is finished in beauty

*English version by Washington Matthews*

# SONG OF THE BALD EAGLE

### *Crow*

we want what is real
we want what is real
don't deceive us!

*Translation by Lewis Henry Morgan*

# SONG OF THE HUMPBACKED FLUTE PLAYER

### *Hopi*

Kitana-po, ki-tana-po, ki-tana-po, ki-tana-PO!
Ai-na, ki-na-weh, ki-na-weh
Chi-li li-cha, chi-li li-cha
Don-ka-va-ki, mas-i-ki-va-ki
Ki-ve, ki-ve-na-meh
HOPET!

*Note*: Kokopelli, the humpbacked flute player, was a fertility spirit who carried seeds in the hump on his back and is often portrayed with a large penis. He scatters those seeds in his wanderings, during which he plays his flute (which creates warmth) and sings. Rothenberg reports that Kokopelli's "song is still remembered, but the words are so ancient that nobody knows what they mean."

# CALENDARS

### Dakota

1. hard moon   2. racoon moon   3. sore eyes moon   4. moon in which the geese lay eggs / moon in which the streams are again navigable   5. planting moon   6. moon in which the strawberries are red   7. moon in which the chokecherries are ripe & the geese shed their feathers   8. harvest moon   9. moon in which wild rice is laid up to dry   10. drying rice moon   11. deer rutting moon   12. moon when deer shed horns

### Tlingit

1. goose month   2. black bear month   3. silver salmon month   4. month before everything hatches   5. month everything hatches   6. time of the long days   7. month when the geese can't fly   8. month when all kinds of animal prepare their dens   9. moon child   10. big moon / formation of ice   11. month when all creatures go into their dens / the sun disappears 12. ground hog mother's moon

### Loucheux

1. moon when dog is cold   2. moon of ice   3. moon of eagles   4. moon in which dog barks   5. moon of the break up of ice / moon of the sea   6. moon of moulting   7. moon of the long day   8. moon of the rutting reindeer   9. moon of the chase   10. moon of warmth   11. moon of mountain goats   12. moon in which the sun is dead

### Carrier

1. moon of the wind   2. moon of the snow storm   3. moon of the golden eagle   4. moon of the wild goose   5. moon of the black bear / moon of the carp   6. moon when they take to the water   7. the buffalo ruts / moon of the land locked salmon   8. moon of the red salmon   9. moon of the bull trout   10. moon of the white fish   11. during its half they navigate / the fat of animals disappears   12. what freezes is covered with bare ice

# TREE OLD WOMAN

### Swampy Cree

She stood close to a tree and wrinkled
her face, TIGHT,
and this was her tree-bark face.
It felt like bark, too, when you ran fingers
over it.

Tree old woman,
even when she was young.

Then her face would smooth out
into a young girl again. Once, after doing
her tree-bark face, she said,
"I *was* a tree and I saw woodpecker
who wanted my head! That's why
I smoothed out my face so quickly!"

We looked up in the trees for that woodpecker,
but it wasn't there. So, our eyes
turned back to her. She was gone too!
We found her in a lake. She was holding on
to some shore reeds
with her legs floating out behind.
She looked up at us WITH THE WRINKLED FACE
OF A FROG! We were certain of it!
Then she smoothed her face out,
saying, "The largest turtle in the world
was swimming for me, thinking I was a frog!
That's why I smoothed my face out
so quickly!"

We didn't even look
for that turtle.

This time we kept our eyes on her
as she went to sit
by an old man, the oldest
in the village.
She sat down next to him.

Their two faces were close together,
and hers began
to wrinkle up again.

*Translation by Howard Norman*

# TEPEHUA THOUGHT-SONG

Thought was

& though it had been
still remains

or it was hardly born when
boys & girls were.

Though they weren't Old Ones
they found their way with it—

so Thought was given them
so life was by their fathers.

When the music starts

it tells about the time Thought entered
it wants to speak about its happiness

to grasp the music way out there
knowing where it is

& knowing where to enter now
once it had gotten where its fathers were
it greeted them.

> *English version by Jerome Rothenberg,*
> *after Charles Boiles*

# SPRING FJORD

*Eskimo*

I was out in my kayak
I was out at sea in it
I was paddling
very gently in the fjord Ammassivik
there was ice in the water
and on the water a petrel
turned his head this way that way
didn't see me paddling
Suddenly nothing but his tail
then nothing
He plunged but not for me:
huge head upon the water
great hairy seal
giant head with giant eyes, moustache
all shining and dripping
and the seal came gently toward me
Why didn't I harpoon him?
was I sorry for him?
was it the day, the spring day, the seal
playing in the sun
like me?

*English version by Armand Schwerner,*
*after Paul-Émile Victor*

# SWEAT-HOUSE RITUAL NO. 1

## *Omaha*

listen    old man    listen
you rock    listen
old man    listen
listen    didn't i teach all their children
to follow me    listen
listen
listen    unmoving time-without-end    listen
you old man sitting there    listen
on the roads where all the winds come rushing
at the heart of the winds where you're sitting    listen
old man    listen
listen    there's short grasses growing all over you    listen
you sitting there living inside them    listen
listen    i mean you're sitting there covered with birdshit    listen
head's rimmed with soft feathers of birds    listen
old man    listen
you standing there next in command    listen
listen    you water    listen
you water that keeps on flowing
from time out of mind    listen
listen    the children have fed off you
no one's come on our secret
the children go mad for your touch    listen
listen    you standing like somebody's house    listen
just like somewhere to live    listen
you great animals    listen
listen    you making a covering over us    listen
saying    let the thoughts of those children live with me & let them love
      me    listen
listen    you tent-frame    listen
you standing with back bent    you over us
stooping your shoulders    you bending over us
you really standing

you saying    thus shall my little ones speak of me
you brushing the hair back from your forehead    listen
the hair of your head
the grass growing over you
you with your hair turning white    listen
the hair growing over your head    listen
o you roads the children will be walking on    listen
all the ways they'll run to be safe    listen
they'll escape    their shoulders bending with age where they walk
walking where others have walked
their hands shading their brows
while they walk & are old    listen
because they're wanting to share in your strength    listen
the children want to be close by your side    listen
walking    listen
be very old & listen

*English version by Jerome Rothenberg,*
*from Alice Fletcher and Francis LaFlesche*

# CROW VERSIONS

1

I am making
    a wind come here

    it's coming

2

Child listen
    I am singing

    with my ear on the ground

    and we love you

                    *by White-arm*

4

If all of me is still there
    when spring comes
    I'll make a hundred poles

    and put something on top
    sun

    for you
    you

right there I'll make a small sweat lodge
    it's cold
    I'll sprinkle charcoal

    at the end of it
    my death

sun
it will all be for you

I want to be still there
that's why I'll do it

thank you

I want to be alive

If my people multiply
I'll make it for you

I'm saying
may no one be sick

so I make it

so

*by Plenty-hawk*


6

He was there
    Old Man Coyote

Water all over the earth
no animals

He looked around
    grabbed

    and there was a little bird

    a swallow
    they say

He told it Go down
  bring earth

  it brought none

Then a crow
  Go down
  get some mud

  it brought none

Wolf
  you bring it

  it brought none

Old Man said
  nothing I can do

  grabbed a duck
  then duck gone

  it's gone

he said to himself it won't be back
  he brought earth

  made this world
  here

  then mud people
  mud man
  mud woman

at that time
  with only that much mud
  that was how

Afterward there was a baby
    a boy

then he had a baby
    a girl

so

    as they say again and again
    now there was
    being born

    more people
    came to be

    you get married
    you make others

*by Medicine-tail*


7

I am climbing
    everywhere is

    coming up

*English versions by W. S. Merwin,*
*after Robert Lowie*

# Nameless Wilds

## W. S. Merwin

(1927–)

W. S. MERWIN TOO WAS SICK AT HEART OVER THE relentless human destruction of planetary life, led by a rapacious America. He was haunted by the poetries of primal cultures, their promise of a more primitive and authentic form of experience, and by grief over the fact that such cultures were rapidly disappearing. As a prolific translator, he ranged capaciously across all of our planet's cultural diversity, but perhaps most important to his own work were his translations from primal cultures (p. 198) and from experimental French and Spanish poets, with their attempts to render deeper and more elemental levels of the psyche. He encountered the insights of ancient China and Buddhism—the emphasis on silence and depths of experience free of language—that would become central to his life in the form of a serious Ch'an practice. Eventually, he left the virulence of modern America (its environmental destruction, its war in Vietnam, its sexist and racist depredations at home and around the world) for a rustic farmhouse in rural France, where he could grow his own food and live closer to the rhythms of natural process.

Well into Merwin's career as a rather conventional poet, these experiences precipitated a fundamental transformation of his work and of poetry itself. His loyalty seemingly slipped beyond the human to the planetary, leading him to reinvent the traditional poetic voice as a uniquely ecopoetic voice. His poems came to speak as something elemental and mysterious and nameless, something primal and almost more silence than speech, more animal or earth than human. Humanness is conscribed by thought and language and names, all of that self-absorbed machinery of thought that precludes *contact* in our day-to-day experience, but Merwin's voice stands outside of that: a presence beyond speech, but which is somehow speaking. A presence that speaks in a more primal grammar: no punctuation; lines following primal rhythms, some long and some short; end-breaks designed to heighten mystery, sometimes following oral breath-rhythms, sometimes frustrating those rhythms and confusing meaning. A presence that takes silence and namelessness as its homeland, that voices a mysterious weave of consciousness and Cosmos in an almost post-apocalyptic sense of human consciousness dying back into the earth. Strange, given that, how beautiful and even comforting the poems are.

This realm of the silent and nameless is a place Ch'an practice cultivates, consciousness dwelling at a level deeper than thought and self and the human, a level where consciousness is integral to everything elemental and nameless, where day-to-day experience is a tissue of *contact*-immediacy. Merwin eventually settled in Hawaii, moving there to study Ch'an with Robert Aitken, a legendary roshi who published numerous books on Ch'an and its literature. Merwin also committed himself there to reforesting a piece of land devastated by toxic agricultural practices, a commitment to replace anger over environmental destruction with a practice of treasuring what is being lost. This impulse is related to the Ch'an insight that enlightenment is always now, in a caressing attentiveness to the ordinary elements of our lives. Perhaps this same impulse is part of the reason Merwin wrote his radical poetry—presented in this chapter—for only about ten years, then returned to a more recognizably human voice. But you can always hear in that later voice echoes of his more radical poetry, its silence and nameless depths.

# KIN

Up the west slope before dark
shadow of my smoke
old man

climbing the old men's mountain

at the end
birds lead something down to me
it is silence

they leave it with me
in the dark
it is from them

that I am descended

# NIGHT WIND

All through the dark the wind looks
for the grief it belongs to
but there was no place
for that any more

I have looked too
and seen only the nameless hunger
watching us out of the stars
ancestor

and the black fields

# THE CALLING UNDER THE BREATH

Through the evening
the mountains approach over the desert
sails from a windless kingdom

silence runs through the birds
their shadows freeze

where are you

where are you where are you
I have set sail on a fast mountain
whose shadow is everywhere

# THE HERDS

Climbing northward
At dusk when the horizon rose like a hand I would turn aside
Before dark I would stop by the stream falling through black ice
And once more celebrate our distance from men

As I lay among stones high in the starless night
Out of the many hoof tracks the sound of herds
Would begin to reach me again
Above them their ancient sun skating far off

Sleeping by the glass mountain
I would watch the flocks of light grazing
And the water preparing its descent
To the first dead

# WORDS FROM A TOTEM ANIMAL

Distance
is where we were
but empty of us and ahead of
me lying out in the rushes thinking
even the nights cannot come back to their hill
any time

    ———

I would rather the wind came from outside
from mountains anywhere
from the stars from other
worlds even as
cold as it is this
ghost of mine passing
through me

    ———

I know your silence
and the repetition
like that of a word in the ear of death
teaching
itself
itself
that is the sound of my running
the plea
plea that it makes
which you will never hear
oh god of beginnings
immortal

    ———

I might have been right
not who I am
but alright
among the walls among the reasons
not even waiting
not seen

but now I am out in my feet
and they on their way
the old trees jump up again and again
strangers
there are no names for the rivers
for the days for the nights
I am who I am
oh lord cold as the thoughts of birds
and everyone can see me

———————

Caught again and held again
again I am not a blessing
they bring me
names
that would fit anything
they bring them to me
they bring me hopes
all day I turn
making ropes
helping

———————

My eyes are waiting for me
in the dusk
they are still closed
they have been waiting a long time
and I am feeling my way toward them

———————

I am going up stream
taking to the water from time to time
my marks dry off the stones before morning
the dark surface
strokes the night
above its way
There are no stars
there is no grief
I will never arrive
I stumble when I remember how it was

with one foot
one foot still in a name

----

I can turn myself toward the other joys and their lights
but not find them
I can put my words into the mouths
of spirits
but they will not say them
I can run all night and win
and win

----

Dead leaves crushed grasses fallen limbs
the world is full of prayers
arrived at from
afterwards
a voice full of breaking
heard from afterwards
through all
the length of the night

----

I am never all of me
unto myself
and sometimes I go slowly
knowing that a sound one sound
is following me from world
to world
and that I die each time
before it reaches me

----

When I stop I am alone
at night sometimes it is almost good
as though I were almost there
sometimes then I see there is
in a bush beside me the same question
why are you
on this way
I said I will ask the stars

why are you falling and they answered
which of us

——————

I dreamed I had no nails
no hair
I had lost one of the senses
not sure which
the soles peeled from my feet and
drifted away
clouds
It's all one
feet
stay mine
hold the world lightly

——————

Stars even you
have been used
but not you
silence
blessing
calling me when I am lost

——————

Maybe I will come
to where I am one
and find
I have been waiting there
as a new
year finds the song of the nuthatch

——————

Send me out into another life
lord because this one is growing faint
I do not think it goes all the way

# THE COLD BEFORE THE MOONRISE

It is too simple to turn to the sound
Of frost stirring among its
Stars like an animal asleep
In the winter night
And say I was born far from home
If there is a place where this is the language may
It be my country

# THE CLEAR SKIES

The clouds that touch us out of clear skies

they are eyes that we lost
long ago on the mountain
and lose
every day on the dark mountain
under clear skies

and because we lose them we say they are old
because they are blind we say
that they cannot find us
that their cloudy gaze
cannot touch us
on our mountain

because we have lost whoever
they are calling
we say that they are not calling
us

## EARLY ONE SUMMER

Years from now
someone will come upon a layer of birds
and not know what he is listening for

these are days
when the beetles hurry through dry grass
hiding pieces of light they have stolen


## EYES OF SUMMER

All the stones have been us
and will be again
as the sun touches them you can feel
sun
and remember waking with no face
knowing that it was summer
still
when the witnesses
day after day are blinded
so that they will forget nothing

# THE ANIMALS

All these years behind windows
With blind crosses sweeping the tables

And myself tracking over empty ground
Animals I never saw

I with no voice

Remembering names to invent for them
Will any come back will one

Saying yes

Saying look carefully yes
We will meet again

# BEGINNING

Long before spring
king of the black cranes
rises one day
from the black
needle's eye
on the white plain
under the white sky

the crown turns
and the eye
drilled clear through his head
turns
it is north everywhere
come out he says

come out then
the light is not yet
divided
it is a long way
to the first
anything
come even so
we will start
bring your nights with you

# DECEMBER AMONG THE VANISHED

The old snow gets up and moves taking its
Birds with it

The beasts hide in the knitted walls
From the winter that lipless man
Hinges echo but nothing opens

A silence before this one
Has left its broken huts facing the pastures
Through their stone roofs the snow
And the darkness walk down

In one of them I sit with a dead shepherd
And watch his lambs

# A CALM IN APRIL

Early mist
mountains like a rack of dishes
in a house I love
far mountains
last night the stars for a while
stopped trembling
and this morning the light will speak to me
of what concerns me

# PROVISION

All morning with dry instruments
The field repeats the sound
Of rain
From memory
And in the wall
The dead increase their invisible honey
It is August
The flocks are beginning to form
I will take with me the emptiness of my hands
What you do not have you find everywhere

# THE DREAM AGAIN

I take the road that bears leaves in the mountains
I grow hard to see then I vanish entirely
On the peaks it is summer

# Meaningless Wilds

## A. R. Ammons

(1926–2001)

M EANING IS MEANINGLESS. IT'S A REALIZATION
remarkable enough that it changes everything, and it is fun-
damental to A. R. Ammons's poetry. Ammons has little patience for the
Western intellectual tradition:

> You would think that after 2500 years we would begin to wonder
> whether or not the framework provided by the discursive in defining
> intellect is sufficient to encounter what we think of as reality. . . .We
> certainly have had enough of trying to explain away reality, because
> we've gotten nowhere, as far as I can tell, in 2500 years.

He preferred the insights of ancient China; and indeed, his career as a
poet began in college when he encountered an exhibition of Chinese
art that included translations of the poems inscribed on paintings.* For
him, the Cosmos is Lao Tzu's Tao (see p. 7), a single vast tissue in con-
stant transformation. And in stark contrast to the Western insistence on
the "discursive in defining intellect," the belief that we can capture the
essence of things through abstract thought and language, Ammons shares
the skepticism of Lao Tzu and the Ch'an masters, who recognized that
language does not connect us with foundational reality (*tzu-jan*), that it

---

* Thanks to Roger Gilbert, Ammons's biographer, for this fact.

only replaces the thusness of reality with our human constructs. However perfectly we describe reality through the languages of science or myth or poetry, reality remains untouched, wholly sufficient and meaningless in and of itself. However immediately and concretely it may refer to reality, language always remains a self-enclosed mental realm; and insofar as we inhabit language, we are ontologically isolated from reality. Lao Tzu recognized this, famously beginning his *Tao Te Ching* with "The Tao you can say is not the perennial Tao" or "The Tao you can call Tao is not the perennial Tao." These insights would seem to preclude poetry at this fundamental level. Ammons's response is the seemingly reckless proposition: "I'm always trying to speak the unspeakable."

Tao, that "unspeakable" tissue, is Ammons's ultimate interest, and he calls it by a variety of names: "formlessness," "whatever is," "the changeless," "the underlying that takes no image to itself," "what, moving, is," "the unstructured sources of our beings." Ammons recognizes nothingness and silence as the most perfect expression of that tissue, and quotes Lao Tzu approvingly: "Nothing that can be said in words is worth saying." But silence alone cannot offer the difficult understanding of dwelling. So Ammons uses words to say what words cannot say, to push language beyond its limits. It is his distinctive ecopoetic project. He weaves together word and silence, knowing and unknowing; for in that weave we can inhabit the vast tissue of Tao, consciousness woven into Cosmos at the deepest level.

"Formlessness," that undifferentiated generative tissue—we cannot experience it directly so long as we are engaged with particular forms. So, quite unlike imagist strategies that establish an immediate mirror-like relation between consciousness and the particular forms of our world, that allow us to think in things themselves, Ammons's poems are always in motion, which is how they create that weave of consciousness and Cosmos. They never settle into any kind of final meaning. Always there at the moment of *contact*, they enact *wu-wei* (see p. 8), moving with the energy of the Cosmos—where nothing holds still, nothing is permanent and nothing fundamentally knowable, where it's all transformation. Spontaneous and improvisational, associative, seemingly effortless, Ammons's *wu-wei* practice is a language that swerves and backtracks, rambles and wanders, always with an anti-poetic challenge to poetic norms. And as with Olson, this embodies Lao Tzu's primal sense of time not as linear, but as an ongoing moment of transformation. Periods are usually replaced by colons, so that rather than stalling at the ends of sentences, the poem's movement is propulsed forward. Precise scientific description of concrete reality (*tzu-jan*) blurs into abstraction, which is soon replaced again by the empirical. The poems range from a few lines to thousands of lines, lines scattered on the page, sometimes short and sometimes long, usually breaking in unpredictable ways so a long prosaic line might be followed by a line made up of only a word or two. And over the body of Ammons's work, each poem feels like another ripple in a larger movement, the mind responding to whatever it encounters at the moment, always provisional, always on its way to the next possibility, the next poem (a fact inadvertently emphasized in his *Collected Poems* where each poem is followed directly on the page by the next). The poems are often self-reflexive, talking about how they work—and so, teaching us how to read them. And they insist that they don't say anything, that the poem is in the music of its motion:

> but the music
> in poems
> is different,
> points to nothing,
> traps no
> realities, takes
> no game, but
> by the motion of
> its motion
> resembles
> what, moving, is—

Ammons's poetry is a more fully realized and consistent manifestation of Olson's poetics: not just mind moving with the energy of the Cosmos (which in Olson generally remains an isolated subjectivity), but engaged with and weaving itself through empirical reality: *tzu-jan* woven through *tzu-jan*. Ammons accepts the "lyrical interference of the ego"—and so, enacts *wu-wei* wholly. An Ammons poem is thought moving the way the tissue of the Cosmos moves, is in fact integral to that tissue. It therefore allows us to experience that tissue directly, enacting unsayable insight much like answers to Ch'an koans. Poetry, then, as a deep-ecological spiritual practice (though Ammons would refuse those labels, like all the other labels one may use to define him). Defying the Western insistence on the "discursive in defining intellect" that generates and perpetuates the self or spirit-center as a locus outside of reality, as the exception to the wildness of the Cosmos, Ammons's poetry returns us to the self as wild, as one more swirl in the unfurling of the Cosmos self

> as it is known
> by galaxy and cedar cone,
> as if birth had never found it
> and death could never end it.

In this, Ammons's poetic practices change the nature of language. No longer is it a "spirit-realm" looking out mimetically on static reality. It is instead part of that reality, elemental: "our own expressiveness is inseparable from all expressiveness," like the sea's expressiveness in "Expressions of Sea Level" (p. 235). And because everything else in the Cosmos is meaningless, the poem is likewise meaningless. Meaning is meaningless; and further, as he declares at the beginning of his book-length poem *Glare*: "meaninglessness/[is] our only meaning." In that meaninglessness, human consciousness is wild again, woven wholly into not just the empirical Cosmos, but into its very sources.

# IDENTITY

    1)    An individual spider web
          identifies a species:

an order of instinct prevails
     through all accidents of circumstance,
        though possibility is
high along the peripheries of
spider

          webs:
          you can go all
        around the fringing attachments

      and find
disorder ripe,
entropy rich, high levels of random,
     numerous occasions of accident:

    2)    the possible settings
        of a web are infinite:

    how does
the spider keep
       identity
    while creating the web
    in a particular place?

    how and to what extent
       and by what modes of chemistry
       and control?

it is
wonderful

how things work: I will tell you
      about it
      because

it is interesting
and because whatever is
moves in weeds
    and stars and spider webs
and known

      is loved:
     in that love,
    each of us knowing it,
    I love you,

for it moves within and beyond us,
      sizzles in
winter grasses, darts and hangs with bumblebees
by summer windowsills:

      I will show you
the underlying that takes no image to itself,
      cannot be shown or said,
but weaves in and out of moons and bladderweeds,
     is all and
    beyond destruction
    because created fully in no
particular form:

      if the web were perfectly pre-set,
      the spider could
   never find
   a perfect place to set it in: and

      if the web were
perfectly adaptable,
if freedom and possibility were without limit,

                    the web would
lose its special identity:

        the row-strung garden web
keeps order at the center
where space is freest (interesting that the freest
                "medium" should
                accept the firmest order)

and that
order
                    diminishes toward the
periphery
        allowing at the points of contact
                    entropy equal to entropy.

# CORSONS INLET

I went for a walk over the dunes again this morning
to the sea,
then turned right along
    the surf
                    rounded a naked headland
                    and returned

    along the inlet shore:

it was muggy sunny, the wind from the sea steady and high,
crisp in the running sand,
        some breakthroughs of sun
    but after a bit

continuous overcast:

the walk liberating, I was released from forms,
from the perpendiculars,
        straight lines, blocks, boxes, binds
of thought
into the hues, shadings, rises, flowing bends and blends
            of sight:

                    I allow myself eddies of meaning:
yield to a direction of significance
running
like a stream through the geography of my work:
    you can find
in my sayings
                    swerves of action
                    like the inlet's cutting edge:
            there are dunes of motion,
organizations of grass, white sandy paths of remembrance
in the overall wandering of mirroring mind:

but Overall is beyond me: is the sum of these events
I cannot draw, the ledger I cannot keep, the accounting
beyond the account:

in nature there are few sharp lines: there are areas of
primrose
          more or less dispersed;
disorderly orders of bayberry; between the rows
of dunes,
irregular swamps of reeds,
though not reeds alone, but grass, bayberry, yarrow, all . . .
predominantly reeds:

I have reached no conclusions, have erected no boundaries,
shutting out and shutting in, separating inside
          from outside: I have
          drawn no lines:
          as

manifold events of sand
change the dune's shape that will not be the same shape
tomorrow,

so I am willing to go along, to accept
the becoming
thought, to stake off no beginnings or ends, establish
          no walls:

by transitions the land falls from grassy dunes to creek
to undercreek: but there are no lines, though
          change in that transition is clear
          as any sharpness: but "sharpness" spread out,
allowed to occur over a wider range
than mental lines can keep:

the moon was full last night: today, low tide was low:
black shoals of mussels exposed to the risk
of air

and, earlier, of sun,
waved in and out with the waterline, waterline inexact,
caught always in the event of change:
    a young mottled gull stood free on the shoals
    and ate
to vomiting: another gull, squawking possession, cracked a crab,
picked out the entrails, swallowed the soft-shelled legs, a ruddy
turnstone running in to snatch leftover bits:

risk is full: every living thing in
siege: the demand is life, to keep life: the small
white blacklegged egret, how beautiful, quietly stalks and spears
    the shallows, darts to shore
        to stab—what? I couldn't
  see against the black mudflats—a frightened
  fiddler crab?

    the news to my left over the dunes and
reeds and bayberry clumps was
    fall: thousands of tree swallows
    gathering for flight:
    an order held
    in constant change: a congregation
rich with entropy: nevertheless, separable, noticeable
  as one event,
    not chaos: preparations for
flight from winter,
cheet, cheet, cheet, cheet, wings rifling the green clumps,
beaks
at the bayberries
  a perception full of wind, flight, curve,
  sound:
  the possibility of rule as the sum of rulelessness:
the "field" of action
with moving, incalculable center:

in the smaller view, order tight with shape:
blue tiny flowers on a leafless weed: carapace of crab:

snail shell:
>pulsations of order
>in the bellies of minnows: orders swallowed,
broken down, transferred through membranes
to strengthen larger orders: but in the large view, no
lines or changeless shapes: the working in and out, together
>and against, of millions of events: this,
>>so that I make
>>no form of
>>formlessness:

orders as summaries, as outcomes of actions override
or in some way result, not predictably (seeing me gain
the top of a dune,
the swallows
could take flight—some other fields of bayberry
>could enter fall
>berryless) and there is serenity:

>no arranged terror: no forcing of image, plan,
or thought:
no propaganda, no humbling of reality to precept:

terror pervades but is not arranged, all possibilities
of escape open: no route shut, except in
  the sudden loss of all routes:

>I see narrow orders, limited tightness, but will
not run to that easy victory:
>still around the looser, wider forces work:
>I will try
  to fasten into order enlarging grasps of disorder, widening
scope, but enjoying the freedom that
Scope eludes my grasp, that there is no finality of vision,
that I have perceived nothing completely,
>that tomorrow a new walk is a new walk.

# REFLECTIVE

I found a
weed
that had a

mirror in it
and that
mirror

looked in at
a mirror
in

me that
had a
weed in it

# STILL

I said I will find what is lowly
        and put the roots of my identity
        down there:
each day I'll wake up
and find the lowly nearby,
        a handy focus and reminder,
a ready measure of my significance,
the voice by which I would be heard
the wills, the kinds of selfishness
        I could
freely adopt as my own:

but though I have looked everywhere,
        I can find nothing
        to give myself to:
        everything is

magnificent with existence, is in
surfeit of glory:
nothing is diminished,
nothing has been diminished for me:

I said what is more lowly than the grass:
        ah, underneath,
        a ground-crust of dry-burnt moss:
        I looked at it closely
and said this can be my habitat: but
nestling in I
found
        below the brown exterior
        green mechanisms beyond intellect
awaiting resurrection in rain: so I got up

and ran saying there is nothing lowly in the universe:
I found a beggar:

he had stumps for legs: nobody was paying
him any attention: everybody went on by:
      I nestled in and found his life:
there, love shook his body like a devastation:
I said
        though I have looked everywhere
        I can find nothing lowly
        in the universe:

I whirled through transfigurations up and down,
transfigurations of size and shape and place:
        at one sudden point came still,
        stood in wonder:
moss, beggar, weed, tick, pine, self, magnificent
        with being!

# EXPRESSIONS OF SEA LEVEL

Peripherally the ocean
marks itself
   against the gauging land
it erodes and
builds:

it is hard to name
the changeless:
speech without words,
   silence renders it:
and mid-ocean,

sky sealed unbroken to sea,
   there is no way to know
the ocean's speech,
intervolved and markless,
breaking against

   no boulder-held fingerland:
broken, surf things are expressions:
the sea speaks far from its core,
far from its center relinquishes the
long-held roar:

of any mid-sea
speech, the yielding resistances
of wind and water, spray,
swells, whitecaps, moans,
   it is a dream the sea makes,

an inner problem, a self-deep
dark and private anguish
   revealed in small,
by hints, to
keen watchers on the shore:

only with the staid land
is the level conversation really held:
only in the meeting of rock and
    sea is
hard relevance shattered into light:

upbeach the clam shell
    holds smooth dry sand,
remembrance of tide:
water can go at
least that high: in

    the night, if you stay
to watch, or
if you come tomorrow at the right time,
you can see the shell caught
again in wash, the

sand turbulence changed,
new sand left smooth: if
the shell washes loose,
flops over,
    buries its rim in flux,

it will not be silence for
a shell that spoke: the
    half-buried back will
tell how the ocean dreamed
breakers against the land:

into the salt marshes the water comes fast with rising tide:
an inch of rise spreads by yards
    through tidal creeks, round fingerways of land:
the marsh grasses stem-logged
combine wind and water motions,
    slow from dry trembling
to heavier motions of wind translated through

cushioned stems; tide-held slant of grasses
    bent into the wind:

    is there a point of rest where
    the tide turns: is there one
    infinitely tiny higher touch
on the legs of egrets, the
skin of back, bay-eddy reeds:
    is there an instant when fullness is,
    without loss, complete: is there a
    statement perfect in its speech:

how do you know the moon
is moving: see the dry
casting of the beach worm
    dissolve at the
delicate rising touch:

that is the
    expression of sea level,
the talk of giants,
of ocean, moon, sun, of everything,
spoken in a dampened grain of sand.

# CASCADILLA FALLS

I went down by Cascadilla
Falls this
evening, the
stream below the falls,
and picked up a
handsized stone
kidney-shaped, testicular, and

thought all its motions into it,
the 800 mph earth spin,
the 190-million-mile yearly
displacement around the sun,
the overriding
grand
haul

of the galaxy with the 30,000
mph of where
the sun's going:
thought all the interweaving
motions
into myself: dropped

the stone to dead rest:
the stream from other motions
broke
rushing over it:
shelterless,
I turned

to the sky and stood still:
Oh
I do

not know where I am going
that I can live my life
by this single creek.

## ATTENTION

Down by the bay I
kept in mind
at once
the tips of all the rushleaves
and so
came to know
balance's cost and true:
somewhere though in the whole field
is the one
tip
I will some day lose out of mind
and fall through.

# Contact Wilds

## *Larry Eigner*

(*1927–1996*)

C ONTACT! CONTACT! WHAT WOULD A LANGUAGE OF *contact* look like, a language that hews as closely as possible to that opening where we see through the assumptions about *who* and *where we are*, free of the self-absorbed machinery of thought? It would be the most minimal of languages, an ecopoetry of the least possible materials — and so, free of the structures of knowing that define us as centers of identity separate from the empirical world around us. Conventional language can say profound and transformative things, but it remains always the language of everyday identity. As we have seen in other poets to varying extents — if you restructure language, more fundamental transformations become possible. That is exactly what happens with Larry Eigner in a radical sense, for he reinvents language, shaping it into that minimal language of *contact*, where consciousness is woven into the Cosmos.

Because *contact* is necessarily lost when even the first word of explanation begins, the greatest poets in this tradition we are tracing may be those who knew better than to write poems at all (a commonplace suspicion among classical Chinese poets). They are of course lost to us, however much we may honor them, but Larry Eigner is a close approximation to those poets, for he reduced poetry to its barest essentials: word and empty space, the first rustle of a mind beginning to construct a *who* and a *where*, and yet never more than a first rustle. Self-identity is conjured from structures of meaning and explanation: phrases, sentences, metaphor, idea, story, etc. But such elements exist in an Eigner poem only in the faintest and most fleeting way. He wrote out of the Cagean premise that "self-assertion (or the isolated I, like anything else enough by itself) is none too interesting, is unlike (self-/) discovery a blind alley." As that "(self-/) discovery," an Eigner poem is made up of whatever happens to occur there in front of him: clouds, trees, ocean, birds. It is the record of perceptions passing through the mirror of empty consciousness—that clarity perfected in Ch'an meditation—perceptions and slight mental events appearing occasionally in that mirror of consciousness with the same status as facts in the world. The two realms, subjective and objective, register as a single field of *tzu-jan* (see p. 8) emergence: occurrence. Momentary coherences appear and quickly disappear, dissolving into word, fragment, transformation in an empty field of simultaneity:

home

fires

burn

walls

meet

stars
naked
cloud
shifting

such sky

all through

the apple

branches

what distance

shades

light

    This is poetry reduced to its least possible materials, stripped down to a
clarity only possible by abandoning those structures of meaning and expla-
nation, the resources of a *who* shaping a *where*. Here, the first five words
appear independently in space, with no apparent relations between them:
*tzu-jan*, simple facts in the world, the facts that just happen to occur, no
spirit-center choosing and ordering them in order to construct meaning
in the form of poetic imagery (hence, a kind of "anti-Imagism"). But read-
ing them, a grammar appears, and possible sentences: "Home fires burn"
and "walls meet," a description of shelter. Or perhaps the scary "home
fires burn walls, meet stars": a destruction of shelter. This is, as Fenollosa
recognized, how Chinese poetry works: imagistic ideograms appearing in
open grammatical space. And so, Eigner practices Pound's ideogrammic
method in a particularly radical way, so radical that a poem's constellation
of image-facts rarely offers meaning in any conventional sense.
    After those first five words, the poem opens into a series of fragmen-
tary moments in space, beginning with the very ambiguous "naked" —
ambiguous because it isn't at all clear what this adjective describes. Is it
fires, or stars, or cloud, or walls? Perhaps the mind in the midst of this
poem/experience? Perhaps the existential exposure after home fires have
burned walls in a kind of elemental betrayal and met the stars?
    An Eigner poem is a meditation. Reading it requires a quiet mind, and it
conspires to conjure that quiet mind, to clarify attention. It slows us down,
empties mind, brings us to the edge of silence where *contact* becomes
possible, where *who* and *where* dissolve into one another. By the end of this
poem, we have reached that edge, and going back to the beginning we see

those first five words as the poem's spatial design suggests: as *tzu-jan*, occurrence, sheer facts emerging from a field of emptiness, existing in and of themselves, liberated by the poem from their usual roles in human systems of meaning-making, and therefore meaningless.

A typical Eigner poem offers even less meaning-making than this one; and so, it is a radical form of ecopoetry, because meaning-making is what isolates consciousness from Cosmos. Instead of meaning-making, an Eigner poem unfurls through moments of transformation, one event replacing another, dissolving any sense of a coherent centered identity writing or reading. There is no sense of an individual mind (Eigner) talking to another individual mind (reader). (In the rare event that "I" appears, it registers as a fact among other facts in the world.) Instead, we as readers inhabit the poem as immediate experience, an immediate experience of *contact* almost unmediated by the structures of identity. This is to experience self and world as mystery, an experience created by the poem's replacement of meaning-making with isolated moments of perception (words) existing in a kind of simultaneity of transformation—that very different, primal sense of time not as linear, but as an ongoing moment of transformation: *tzu-jan*, occurrence appearing of itself. And with *tzu-jan* comes Tao, the Cosmos as a generative tissue, for Eigner's poetic form enacts this generative cosmos in which things appear out of emptiness in and of themselves, perfectly mysterious, only to be replaced by the next thing: a radically different experience of time. An Eigner poem is truly "talk of mysteries," for it makes no attempt to invest the world with meaning. Instead it simply inhabits the empty-mind openness of *contact*, of consciousness woven back into Cosmos.

                things
                    stirring
                together

                        the wind

                            fly

                    objects

                        birds, shove
                out

                            thermals

the wind's
    tune

how constructed
   things are

        the instrument

        now we know


        listen

        light comes through it and

        water

        shakes

    clouds    rain down trees    fog

now

here

too

elsewhere

what

next

clouds

down

beyond the sky

and one

gust

the rain and the stars

        in the head
        in the head

          beaches

        slow clouds, the dark

the sound

in its reach

cold

north
   is

it ended

now or

something

different

meaning

leaves

a mask

puddles

street
signs

the branches

in the eyes

sparrows

how far

good and bad

time goes

leaves changing shadows


the wind fails    what paths


I fight nothing
there are no weapons


separate clouds

traveling   in the years


the sun, depths,
varying, mass

grief     dry the

                council

      far away

     inveterate        interest

      some dust

        the stars are a million pieces

              some million a million

         people suffer the end

driftwood

the sands

a tree spreads

dirt is

hard grains

Head full
of birds     the languages
of the world
     switching the scenery     the same
     old things

          a crow     momentary
          thicknesses of the air
          are hills     shadows
          below waver
          some clearness     now these trees

               level the lawn
               across the street

          the sun there
                    shift the world up out

                    whistle in snow

shadowy

gesticulations

on the lawn


young tree
trunks
a little in the sun

leaf
shapes
across them too



beautiful

the light is

all one way

after

noon

where it falls



most of the earth

unknown

to us


clouds are idle


spaces

the sound

        sea through the horizon
     under the stand of trees

  it comes by on the wind

    flat and round
    earth and sky

earth     air

a grave

water is more than land

the exotic,     strange

step

such light traps

the moon

shadows

bullets

whales' music around the world

dream    the sea


make, man
        breath felt

   find the
    speeds


       living

       slow

       and the steady

       wind

the way you go

        far from one another

    circles

            neighborhood
                  trees
               spread out

           corners

              how conscious

                young or old

                  birds there are

                    clouds float

                      in the moist air

Quiet grass

*(after Bashō*

still air

rocks

the locust

cries

# Mosaic Wilds

## Ronald Johnson

### (1935–1998)

A S THE MEDIUM OF THOUGHT, LANGUAGE IN AND OF
itself structures mind and self-identity at a more fundamen-
tal level than the content language conveys, and it thereby structures our
relationship to the world. *Who are we, where are we*: our conventional as-
sumptions about Thoreau's questions involve mind as a self-enclosed spirit-
center speaking about a world outside of itself, taking the world as an object
of its attention, and those assumptions are structured by a language that
is linear and logical, discursive and narrative (the spirit-center language
that was formalized and spiritualized in the traditional language of poetry
that Pound challenged: its heightened diction, rhyme and meter, poetic
embellishment, etc.). As we have seen, reinventing language seems poten-
tially the most fundamental way of opening consciousness to *contact* and
reinventing the answers to Thoreau's existential questions. And indeed, for
most poets in this ecopoetic tradition, how they restructure language is at
least as important as what they say. In fact, it is often more important. This
is the revolution of Olson and Cage: it isn't what they *say* with language,
but what they *do*, what they *enact*. Ronald Johnson is yet another exemplar
of this radical strategy, using collage techniques to construct poems free of
the traditional organizing self, poems that open consciousness in a radical
way to the possibility of *contact*.

Johnson's great achievement is a book-length poem entitled *Ark*, which sounds in his description very like that moment of *contact* and the attempt there to begin answering Thoreau's questions anew: "to start all over again, attempting to know nothing but a will to create, and matter at hand." But *Ark* is prefigured by *Radi Os*, a book-length poem in which he dismantles Milton's *Paradise Lost* (epic monument of the Western tradition) by erasing most of the text to create a new poem. The transformation is apparent even in the title, where *Paradise Lost* (with all its theological reference) becomes through Johnson's process of erasure: *Radi Os*, meaning (among a number of possibilities, including the comically gratuitous "radios" and the geometric "radius," as in planets or orbits) something akin to "Light Bone." Or perhaps, reading *Os* as plural of the circle O: "Radiant Circles," as in sun and stars, planet and moon. Milton's archly poetic language and grand theological drama with its Christian cosmological scheme including the assumption of self as a soul, that alien-being here on earth, and the idea of earth as merely a proving ground where souls play out their drama of redemption—*Radi Os* transforms all of that into voiceless fragments of thought scattered through an open field of silence, into the wide-open space of consciousness itself, space where the self-absorbed machinery of thought opens to a more primal and immediate experience of itself and the world:

the O

      Of

        wonder,

```
                              circumference
        Hung on    shoulders like the moon, whose
                    optic glass
        At evening, from the top
                       new
                               globe
```

Of some great

        burning
         azure;

             vaulted

           Forms,
              autumnal leaves
       where

              winds Orion

   iris

             wheels.

              all the hollow deep

      the Flow

    To slumber
    Or
       adore              ,
                 the flood

    Transfix us
    Awake,

    Upon the wing, as

    The collage effect created by the constellated fragments in *Radi Os* sprawls to a vast scale in *Ark*, Johnson's "mosaic of Cosmos." *Ark* includes anything and everything: all dimensions of empirical reality and human culture (facts as well as textual fragments) and all types of language: discursive prose, high and low diction, fragmented, lyrical, philosophical, scientific, serious, humorous. Using titles like "Foundations" and "Beams," "Spires" and "Arches," *Ark* is constructed as a kind of architectural fantasy, but that structure has little apparent connection with the poem's actual content. What matters is that the collage form operates at every scale: the poem has ninety-nine sections, each of which is an independent fragment usually unrelated to those around it in terms of form and content; each section is itself constructed as collage, with disparate fragments coexisting simultaneously; and each line is often made of discontinuous elements. In *Ark*, Johnson extends Pound's "ideogrammic method," realizing its potentials as Pound never did. And in this form we find again Lao Tzu's primal sense of time as an ongoing generative moment (see p. 8), a simultaneity of transformation, as we do in *Radi Os*.

It is clear Johnson's poetic thought incorporates, perhaps unknowingly, those ancient Chinese insights handed down via Fenollosa/Pound and others in this ecopoetic tradition, and that otherwise infused artistic culture in America during his active years. The fundamental realization in Ch'an meditation, for instance, that we are separate from the thoughts and memories that define identity (see p. 9), that we are instead the empty awareness ("empty mind") that watches identity rehearsing itself in those ongoing thoughts and memories. Rather than organizing experience around a lyric *I*, Johnson's collage form replicates that structure revealed in meditation, creating a form in which the linear language of the rational self is replaced with open-form consciousness as an organic dimension of the Cosmos. The effect is also very like Ch'an koan practice and its riddles intended to break up the conventional structure of thought, for it cultivates consciousness not as a self-enclosed intellect looking out on and contemplating a foreign world, but as a mirror-deep opening into that world. The elements of the collage appear not as props in some human-centered discourse, but in and of themselves as revelation, as a "polyphony of epiphanies" (in Johnson's words). For Johnson, too, emptying self to a mirror-deep clarity that attends to things (*tzu-jan*: that "polyphony of epiphanies") is crucial, is a way of belonging fundamentally to the Cosmos. And Johnson pushes that ecopoetic insight further, for he intends his collage form to create the sense of consciousness (eye and mind) as a creation of the Cosmos, as a site where the Cosmos looks out at, contemplates, and expresses itself: "after a long time of light, there began to be eyes, and light began looking with itself," "the eye may be said to be sun in other form," "mind is a revelation of matter."

Johnson spent several years reading Thoreau's *Journals* as a kind of spiritual/artistic practice, because he wanted to "sharpen [his] eye and how it intersects with text." As we saw in Cage, the *Journals* are perhaps Thoreau's most radical work, almost free of the Western assumptions shaping his Transcendentalism, and remarkably they too replicate those crucial Chinese insights. In them, the self-absorbed thought-process of an inquiring and organizing self is largely replaced with the world itself (*tzu-jan*), for the *Journals* as literary self-expression are so relentlessly about simply recording/expressing what he encounters in the world, about describing and inhabiting the world, caressing and contemplating and celebrating it. So there is a kind of reversal in which the objective world becomes subjective content and expression. The *Journals* describe a daily practice of *contact*. And in this, Thoreau's eye and mind become wholly a part of the Cosmos in a sense not unlike what Johnson and Taoist/Ch'an thought intend. This sense of belonging is deepened dramatically in section 74 of *Ark* (p. 281), where Johnson creates one of his scintillating collages from fragments of the *Journal*. It is an example of how *Ark* extends Thoreau's strategy in a radical way, for in it the language of mosaic dissolves all trace of self and self-expression, replacing it with the things of the world. And more radical versions of this strategy can be found in "ARK 37" (p. 279), which constructs poetic self-expression from fragments of Peterson's *Field Guide to Western Birds*, descriptions of birds and their calls, or "Beam 18" (p. 276) in which the inked imprint of a hand speaks where the inked imprint of text normally would. *Ark*'s mosaic of epiphanies creates a celebratory perception of the Cosmos as "an organism spirally closed on itself, into the pull of existence,"

one being, surround in bloom
flow essential seed
portal system Milky Way

. . .

organism omnipotent


poised in flesh

Consciousness in *contact*, wholly open to *tzu-jan*, the ten thousand things in perpetual transformation: again, this entails necessarily a recognition of the Cosmos as a generative ("flow essential seed") organism, as Tao; and together with that, a recognition of oneself as an integral part of that organic whole:

> The Mind & Eye, the solar system, galaxy
> are spirals coiled from periphery
> —i.e. Catherine Wheels—
> of their worlds.
> Whorls.

BEAM 1

Over the rim
body of earth                    rays exit sun
rest to full velocity to eastward pinwheeled in a sparrow's

eye
—Jupiter compressed west to the other—

wake waves on wave in wave striped White Throat song

along the reversal of one
contra-
centrifugal
*water to touch, all knowledge*

as if a several silver
backlit in gust.

All night the golden fruit fell softly to the air,
pips ablaze, our eyes skinned back.
Clouds loom below. Pocked moon fills half the sky. Stars
comb out its lumen
horizon
in a gone-to-seed dandelion
as of snowflakes hitting black water, time, and again,

then dot the plain
186,282 cooped up angels tall as appletrees

caryatid
one sudden tide of day

O

wide bloom the pathed earth yawn
on purpose porpoised pattern

this reeled world whistling joist its polished fields of sun
pulse race in a vase of beings, bearings
all root fold forms upon
to center eternity
or enter it
*instruments of change.*


and bareback as Pegasus guess us

# BEAM 4

The human eye, a sphere of waters and tissue, absorbs an energy that has come ninety-three million miles from another sphere, the sun. The eye may be said to be sun in other form.

It is part of a spectrum of receptors, and if we could only "see" more widely the night sky would be "brighter" than the moon. Matter smaller than the shortest wavelength of light cannot be seen.

Pressure on the surface of an eye makes vision, though what these same pressures focus to the radial inwardness of a dragonfly in flight is unimaginable. Through pressure also, the head-over-heels is crossed right-side-up, in eye as camera. (It is possible to take a cow's eyeball and thin the rear wall of it with a knife, fit it front forward in a tube, and the tube pointed at an elm will image an upside-down elm.)

The front of the eye is a convex glass, alive, and light bent through its curve strikes a lens. This lens is behind an iris—pushing it into the shape of a volcano. In light, the iris appears as a rayed core of color, its center hole dilating dark to day, transformed instantly into what man's twinned inner hemispheres call sight.

The retina is its bowl-shaped back—the cones at retinal center growing through intersections with rods, toward rods at the rim. Through this mesh, ray seizes ray to see. In the rods there is a two-part molecule that is unlinked by light. One quantum of light unlinks one molecule, and five rods are needed to perceive the difference. Some stars are at this threshold, and can only be seen by the sides of the eyes. The eye can see a wire .01 inch in diameter at a distance of 100 yards. The retina itself seeks equilibrium.

Though to look at the sun directly causes blindness, sight is an intricately precise tip of branched energy that has made it possible to measure the charge of solar storm, or to calculate nova. It is possible that all universe is of a similar form.

Our eyes are blue for the same reason sky is, a scattering of reflectors: human eyes have only brown pigment.

In the embryo two stalks push from the brain, through a series of infoldings, to form optic cups. Where the optic cup reaches surface, the surface turns in and proliferates in the shape of an ingrowing mushroom. The last nerve cells to form are those farthest from light.

If I sit at my table and look at the shaft of light which enters a glass filled with water—and exits rainbow—then move my head to the left, the shaft and glass move right, and the window behind them, left. If I stand up and step to the table, the glass at its edge moves downward, while the far end of the table, and the window with it, rise straight up in the air.

No one knows the first man to stare long at a waterfall, then shift his gaze to the cliff face at its side, to find the rocks at once flow upward. But we have always known the eye to be unsleeping, and that all men are lidless Visionaries through the night. Mind & Eye are a logarithmic spiral coiled from periphery. This is called a "spiral sweep"—a biological form which combines (as do galaxies) economy with beauty. (We define "beauty" from symmetrical perceptions . . .

-------------

After a long time of light, there began to be eyes, and light began looking with itself. At the exact moment of death the pupils open full width.

## BEAM 5, THE VOICES

the l∞m, the x of the instant
looped to time:  windmill-ply of the plenum, laced
ion


eon
:the actuals, like kingfishers
flashing across pools:  minnow beneath flicker:
image to image:
*that-which-consumes and*
—blaze within blaze within blaze—


*that-which-gives-light*:
"the quick, the ag-ile, Ag-nis, ig-nis"
center/circumference in


one


:the outside in a nutshell:


*out magnifying*
*being*
:


c i r c
l e c i
r c l e


o
m o n


*i n* m *i n d i n*


a   e   a   e   a   e   a   e   a   e
w   v   w   v   w   v   w   v   w   v

eyeyeye

.

form from form from form from form

"play'd by the picture of No-body"

*whose bright stripes & broad stars*

pinpointeddyshuttlecrossroadssword

(a-hinged-magnetic-up-and-down-on)

all a bowed honeycomb space become

*Music, anatomy—an atomed Euridice*
as if of fireflies in relief
to turning earth
*&*
thunder, cymbal mazed in timpani of smattering,
arm's electron's long way
back

*radius at which the shock wave relaxes*
*(30° above and below*
*bisect spark)*

*

AND THEN THE THREEFOLD TREEFIRE STROKE-IN-STROKE
AGAIN
—obliquity to the ecliptic—

"bear" (Polar) among the asphodel, singing Bach's Unaccompanied
Cello.

Ear (solar) in Bosch of metanoias—nose to nose Is, Is, Is
(noise)

Polyphony of epiphanies

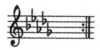

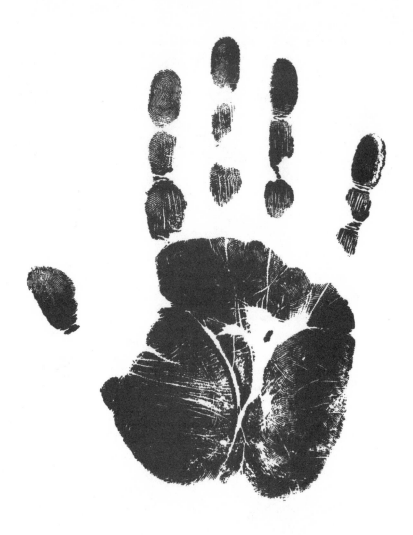

## BEAM 24

earthearthearth
earthearthearth
earthearthearth
earthearthearth
earthearthearth
earthearthearth

"any piece of counterpoint includes
a silent part
for the rhythmic movements of heart and
lungs"

*(lilacs)*

here,
everywhirr
perfect welter acting like generators
*candelulae* parallel
triad *iridae*
Elohim all but invisible, bushes humming of them
susurrus to some oncoming moth in scallop
far unblurred Pleiades:
. . . there *and* there *and* there . . .


"stone lacking all weight"
hunched among the shouldered shuddered things, wings
dizzying into full
sprigged lilac
prestidigitation of one long run errant grace
of harnessing seeming
as evenings a thrush transforms its song
Archaean
earth, still crouched at seed


firstways
*winding as a snake does into the sun*
of speckled loom
unexpecteder than darkness
itself into its radiance's dance, or Hymn spun upon
some literally "rhyme" with men
punned then with the blasted Milky Way, that paths of salt
with time we lumber up
flesh last

# ARK 37, SPIRE CALLED PROSPERO'S SONGS TO ARIEL

*Constructed in the form of a quilt*
*from Roger Tory Peterson's*
A Field Guide to Western Birds


*hear hear hear hear*
*see-see-see*
"upcurled" uttered like a mallet driving a stake
a tick of white, pale buff
constantly changing speed and direction
*immutabilis*
with an air-splitting stitch at the "focus"
"dead-leaf" pattern
in falling diminuendo blending into a broad terminal band of
"code"


low
"dissonances through dissonances through dissonances"
dark-winged Solitary
with a scythelike *check-check-check*
*sewing-machine motion* blood-red to the zoned
*magnificens*
with a center of slower winding
trying to sing like a Canary
in higher orchard
*killy killy killy* great yellow bill


*quark* "frozen"
("like a sparrow dipped in raspberry juice")
in rhythm of a small ball bouncing to a standstill
nestling *flammeus*
closed ellipse with diagonal axis
garden
bordered by blue-stem ethereal prairie
split-second

"Dancing" Cascade Mts.
or frail saucer in conifer

silent
barred crosswise streaked lengthwise
speculum *borealis*
Turnstone white, ochre, cerulean, cog the deep (from above)
Stilt
Great Plains to equator
(clockwork) across Oceans of the
laterally
*a-ring-a-ring-a-ring-a* at wheeling anchor
sawedged image

---

pale ghost-bird of the inner eyrie
silvery over and over
body in strong light, radial
at a distance, only the hollow long-drawn *whoooooooo*
*tooit-wit* winnowing an almost touching elsewhere
in bright yellow lines, twinkling flight to flesh at "window"
"eyed on back of head" at night in spring
in endless succession
as it walks
the rip-tide *paradisaea*

to corners
Blue Goose, in lemon-colored shade
patterning beyond the pale
grass cup in briar
loosed crease in the summer, streams punctuated by daylight
the glass reveals basket-like sparkles of margin
or circumpolar seed seen in sky
violet eyelets in olive
rootling
in wide circles

# ARK 74, ARCHES VIII

*from Thoreau's Journals*


"and something more I saw
left off understanding, around bend
encircling world

Words lie like boulders on a page
woods black as clouds,
blood durable as aqueduct

no surface bare long—
earth covered deep alphabet
this spring laid open with my hoe,

down stream, eyes leveled at you
assume a true sphericity
and bay the moon

multiply deeds within, a cynosure
that every star might fall
into its proper place

being, the great explainer
as if the earth spoke
and heavens crumpled into time

vast glow-worm in fields of ether
as if answered its end,
tail curled about your vitals

sea of mowing, seeing no bottom
leaves ply and flowing fill up path
and thunder near at hand

like summer days seen far away
golden comb, successive lines of haze
set fire to the edges

a crow's wing in every direction,
very deep in the sod
bursting a myriad barrier

as if a cavern unroofed
this great see-saw of brilliants,
oclock strikes whippoorwill

swayed as one, from I know not what
see stars reflected
in the bottom of our boat

chandeliers of darkness
I saw sun shining into like depths,
both planet and the stubble

within compass of a spark
the flute I now hear
on pinnacle, to the end of days

Wing horse, the veery trill
go about search echo
mountains already left these shores

I look under the lids of time,
left without asylum
to gather a new measure

through aisles of ages
art, every stroke of the chisel
enter own flesh and bone

without moving a finger,
turning my very brain
reflected from the grass blades"

# Origin Wilds

## *Gustaf Sobin*

(1935–2005)

G USTAF SOBIN IS AN ARCHAEOLOGIST OF LANGUAGE, of consciousness. Although born and raised in America, he lived his adult life in the Luberon Mountains of southern France, a region where landscape feels alive with layers of ancient cultures: Paleolithic and Neolithic, Bronze Age and Iron Age, Ligurian, Celtic, Roman. There, Sobin wandered fields littered with Neolithic arrowheads and potsherds, bronze earrings, Gallo-Roman bath tiles, studying and thinking down through those cultural levels toward the blank origins from which they grew. For him, words are physical facts obdurate as arrowheads and potsherds, and yet alive. They are physical configurations of air or script, objects living at once today and at the beginnings of language. And they emerge out of landscape the way cultural relics like arrowheads emerge in fieldland after rain, or the way plants bloom, and it is for Sobin an ongoing miracle:

*that*

*each thing, as it's*
*uttered,*
*out of*
*its*

*breath,*
*smoldering, bud!*

There is in Sobin, too, a return to the primitive. Often emphasizing the oral, he reaches for a language that operates as it did in the Paleolithic, before it became the medium of a spirit-center, a mimetic inside looking out on the empirical outside. Sobin suggests this transformation to the mimetic arose during the Neolithic, when humans began controlling nature in the form of domesticated plants and animals, the storage and accumulation of grain (beginning of individual wealth), thereby separating themselves from the

> inseparable, from that level of consciousness that admits to no severance between the animate and the inanimate, between the self and the inextricable fabric of so much surrounding phenomena. . . . Bit by bit, they would come to take their distance from those earliest rocks, winds, stars, those immeasurable expanses of which they once felt themselves an integral part.

For Sobin, this breach between human and "nature" was consummated when originally pictographic languages became alphabetic. His interest in pictographic language maintaining a primal integration of thought and reality is a first connection to China, established through the Fenollosa/Pound essay (and everything implicated below the surface there) and continuing in his translation of Henri Michaux's *Ideograms in China*. Alphabetic language represents a complete withdrawal of thought from the world, because the relationship is no longer pictographic directness but abstract and arbitrary. And so,

> within the tight weave of an ecological fabric, a rent suddenly appears. Between humankind and nature, a sense of rupture, removal, separation replaces that of an essential, deep-seated unity.

Sobin proposes poetry as a return to the archaeological beginnings of language and culture and consciousness, where the breach between thought and landscape has not yet opened, where words are emerging from and vanishing into their empty origins, where the poet is mere "instrument" of those words. For him, poetry begins in the precise perception of landscape, *tzu-jan*: momentary perception and a lifetime of perception. A poem emerges like any other occurrence in the process of *tzu-jan*: it grows out of that landscape as a "teasing of / sound out / of // substance" that can "bring a boulder to // tremble in the wrapt / tissues of a / breath." And it moves with an associative energy, that movement of *wu-wei* (see p. 8). In this process, it is not Sobin who speaks, that individual personality as a separate entity, but rather the landscape speaking itself: landscape as silence, as origin. Indeed, more and more through Sobin's work the poem actually addresses the poet as a "you." What may seem at first a cloying posture, reveals itself to be in fact a deep philosophical statement, for now the poet is quite literally not speaking the poems. Instead, it is origin speaking, landscape or *tzu-jan* or Tao speaking, just as it is in a Chinese poem where the wide-open minimal grammar allows ideograms to emerge out of the absence suffusing a poem.

A Sobin poem doesn't try to *say* things in the conventional sense, and trying to read it that way only leads to confusion, a sense that it is little more than over-wrought talk about language and writing. Instead, as we've seen with other post-Olson poets, it *does* things. Earth become the air of speech (as an early book title announces: *The Earth as Air*), a Sobin poem is a pilgrimage to that origin place, slowly opening its silence: not as vanished past, but as present possibility. It dwells there, resisting that (inevitable) step away into the mimetic, for with that step comes the separation of thought and landscape that establishes thought as a separate spirit-realm looking out on that landscape, opening "that exile we'd come to call self-hood, individuation."

A Sobin poem inhabits, really, a Paleolithic place where origins are everywhere a part of immediate experience, where boulder as thing and boulder as word arise from the same source and have the same ontological status. And so, mind as *wu-wei*: thought moving quite literally as *tzu-jan*. Without the naming of language, existence is a single undifferentiated tissue. It is only when a name appears that an individual thing is separated out from that single tissue: when the word "tree" is first spoken in recognition of the presence a tree forces onto consciousness, the tree itself is defined as an entity separate from everything else. Sobin often describes this origin moment in terms of air being shaped into meaning (word), an entirely physical process free of the metaphysics implicit to the spiritualized linguistic realm created by mimetic language. And as origin place where name and thing create one another, it is the site where a Sobin poem operates. Here we can understand at a deeper level the miracle Sobin finds in this, for where there is no mimetic relation between thing and word, it is not the poet that speaks, but the thing itself indistinguishable from the poet:

> *that*
>
> *each thing, as it's*
> *uttered,*
> *out of*
> *its*
>
> *breath,*
> *smoldering, bud!*

That primal breach of self-identity from the undifferentiated tissue of earth, driven by the Neolithic domestication of nature and alphabetic language: Sobin associates it with the transition from a gynocentric culture to an androcentric culture. For Sobin it was an epochal loss. That "matricular" culture was "virilized" and replaced, perhaps,

> but it's not altogether certain that this culture and the profound deposits it left within the human psyche could, in fact, be replaced. For at an operative level, there'd be nothing, absolutely nothing, with which to replace it. It constitutes foundation itself.

Here Sobin is describing Tao, the Cosmos as a single female ontological tissue, generative origin shaping itself into individuated things. His poetry, too, is generated by that origin-tissue — and so, it is a poetry of primal dwelling. It is the selfless voice reifying origin as a sacred place, generative and female. It does this in an antique and heightened language of newly invented sacred ritual, a language that flaunts its difference from our everyday utilitarian (mimetic) language, announcing in its strangeness that it is earth itself speaking. A Sobin poem speaks not only with a recherché vocabulary and tight rhythms, but also with its own dense internal rhyming of assonance and alliteration. And this language of Sobin's ritual moves as a "continuous becoming"—and so, enacts its belonging to a generative source, a further return to a Taoist/Paleolithic cosmology that is female and generative:

> mother of no one, as
> woman you
>> enter, occupy nothing, but stand, water-
> slick in the midst of these pitted
>>> whispers, no one's, once
>>>> again.

It is in this sacred place that self and world and language generate one another. And here again we find that primal sense of time not as linear, but as an ongoing generative moment, a simultaneity of transformation enshrined in the collage and associative structure of a Sobin poem. For Sobin, this place is inexhaustibly mysterious, something he feels compelled to explore in poem after poem. In doing this, he is constantly opening language (thought) into silence, for that silence beyond language is the generating origin: origin of language, self, and world. After long acquaintance with the Taoist/Ch'an ideas suffusing the avant-garde tradition, Sobin's "enlightenment moment" as a poet came when he read François Cheng's *Chinese Poetic Writing*, a deep account of the Chinese poetic language, its philosophical foundations and implications. With his emptiness and silence, his push past language into origins, his sense of the generative, Sobin intends to create the very place that Taoist/Ch'an practice aspires to, even while struggling with the limitations of the West's materials, its philosophical assumptions, language, etc. And it is the place of Thoreau's *contact*, that place so deep *who* and *where we are* become indistinguishable and unsayable. There, we may inhabit "what our own words aspire, reach towards, as if to imbue themselves with the sonorous luster of their own origins."

A Sobin poem holds this origin moment open, moving there in *contact*, while at the same time trying to explain what it's doing (that unavoidable necessity). But always, even in its explaining, the poem remains wholly elusive, moving in the margins of language, beyond language, where

> whatever utters,
> utters nothing, really.    and makes of that

nothing —lyric— its
only
measure.

This locates Sobin himself somewhere in the generative interstices of language, which is the place where the self-absorbed machinery of thought ends and *contact* is possible. We live in an age of certainty and scientific explanation, and

> as a result, we've grown estranged from origins, deprived of even the vaguest glimpses of those first, founding landscapes. . . . It's as if the dark, floating universe from which humankind has always drawn solace and the impalpable reflection of its own deepest identities has entirely vanished.

A Sobin poem opens a "talk of mysteries," a force field of wonder and query and unknowing. It begins somewhere already in process (often marked by ellipses), as if its beginnings were lost, thereby suffusing itself in silent/unsayable origin. It is often fragmentary, or otherwise full of empty interstice. The language is always provisional, decontextualized, conditional, incomplete, full of words like *as if, might, would, could*. It revels in a vocabulary of vanishing: *vestige, relic, obfuscated, elision, obliterated, nothing, extinguished, dismantled, empty, dissolving, invisible, illegible, abolished, nothing*. And the poet himself, that first-person lyric "I," is absent. Hence, as in a Chinese poem with its empty grammar, language (thought, identity) is perpetually vanishing into the silence around and through it, the silence of origins, which is nothing other than unspoken landscape itself: "liminal / landscapes of the all surrounding *isn't*." In a Sobin poem, "sound . . . abuts silence. Murmur, emptiness. Speech, the inarticulate expanses by which we're surrounded." And so, its ritual movement

> might bring us onto an ontological level of reasoning in which—at its very limits—we might encounter traces of our own long since absconded identity.

Here is dwelling as integral to Tao at the deepest levels of identity, Tao as origin-tissue. It is the dwelling of *contact* in which we inhabit a place prior to *who* and *where*, a place in which, again: language, self, and world generate one another out of an always mysterious and magically generative emptiness. With his complex ecopoetic strategies, Sobin's is a spiritual practice weaving consciousness and Cosmos together at such levels of origin that he could begin his final poem like this:

only written in white would the world, at last, become legible.

# FOURTEEN IRISES FOR J. L.

there, blossoming once again, like blown
goblets, the irises in their annual
     ovulations.   yes, emptiness, at
  last, enveloped, inscribed.   is there anything, indeed, but
       emptiness?   but emptiness, at last, en-
                veloped? inscribed?

-------

   . . . one color
follows upon another like
     polyphonic voices: last week, violet, and
  this, a rubbed mahogany, freckled rose, recalling
       worlds —voices— you've never known.

-------

   . . . like so
many stubby paintbrushes, they
    burst —turbaned— into splashed
panels, running murals (a breath as
        if perishing in the
          very exercise of its scales).

-------

  no, it's not the irises that
return, each spring, but
    ourselves.  ourselves —cyclical— who've entered the
sign, and stoop, now, before
      them: tenuous altars to our own
          tenuous passage.

all irises, finally,
kaleido-
scopic; with each
in-
finitesimal turn, a
fresh

conceit.    god-
blossom, lightning-

root, verb on which,
germinal, the
air it-

self's as if
ir-
idized.

---

   like those glazed, in-
voluted tissues on their tall, un-
     wavering stems, we, too, as if
perch, alighting —as we have— amongst phonemes,
      polyphones: what tell us, each
              instant, to our fingertips.

---

   came late.    even later, now, *la*
*langue d'oc* having all
    but vanished, remained the irises, the troubadours'
lightning roses, blue
        as thunder in the dark thunder's
            *dissoulucioun.*

where dew slips,
icy
pearl, from its

petal, the
tall stalk

scarce-
ly trembles. . . .

—————

irises, really, are nothing more
than the frozen frames of an otherwise
    invisible drift, our relentless
elision past.    what they —heraldic,
                    voluptuous— would arrest.

—————

how each of these blossoms —these
volutes— lapping ogival, in-
    scribe a void.    oh ours, that hollow, that
        heart, that inherent omission: doom blooming
                from the rhizomes up.

—————

drafted, the petals get blown, now,
across paper.    their deep
    scrolls, rolled tabernacles, little more
        than scribbled deposits.    chimeric hoards.

—————

(*gothic*)

death, and these,
our ever
more
ephemeral re-

sponses, their
fluttering
chalices (faience
the

skull dreamt. . . ).

———————

. . . way that the irises drift, now, be-
neath yours.    current in which —wind-
        barges— they'd enter, perhaps, your
    very dreams.    there, before dissolving (so much
        grammatical particle) might billow.    writhe vibrant.

———————

a white chair, its legs caught
in tall stalks
    of white iris, was what, finally,
    remained.    monologue in which, abandoned
                        to those immensities, each
                        of us murmur.

# A PORTRAIT OF SORTS IN MID-MARCH

high over the charred bars of the
    vineyards, a
moon sips
at its own lozenge.    you, too, as
if

thin, self-
dissolve, leaving little more, now,
than that mask you'd
made, its

breathing sheaths: what you'd tapped,
fashioned, perforated into
some-

thing so utterly transparent that
not even you, now,
needed to

ad-
mit to yourself.    bulk without
body, moving over the
burnt

thistles, had you reached, at long
last, the

perfect consistency?    the same weight
as the weeds?    as the
onion stalks you'd
offer —that

very instant— to the abolished face
of the
in-
visible?

# OF AIR AUGMENTED

. . . was air rushing through air that, each
time, solidified sound,
freckled the
still-

seething shadows with
sign, signature, the very stigmata, you'd
called them, of
semblance it-

self. would swell, wouldn't you, to those
sudden

complicities; watch the rocks as if knot on
so
many successive
conjugates. here, where fingers, whole

hearts get blown into the animate, an entire
landscape, this
very

instant, settles (orchard,
windbreak and battlement) within the
singular
respiration of its

disparate parts. here's only
here, you'd

written, in the ganging of its particles, in a
sudden
gust of the meticulously ar-

ticulated.

# THE ARCHEOLOGIST: A BROKEN DICTATION

*la Grotte de l'Escale*


. . . had never been further, you'd
told us; never before
taken the
full measure of 'origins,' you'd
said (your words, already, tattering in mid-

air; reaching us, now, only in so
much

semantic particle. 'glacier,' for instance,
then, weeks
later, something
about roses. 'roses,' you'd said, as
if, having ventured —yes, already— into an
aftermath of

roses, only the utterance, now, as if
subsisted, and even
that, only in splinters —yes, these

brief,
intermittent sparks).


~


itinerary, then, if,
indeed, there were one; if, that
is, one
might have assumed
some kind of sequence, unravelling, other than
that, say, the

fates played, ineluctable. would
sleep, wouldn't you, your
eyes

opened wide on a world without shadows. there,
where doors never closed, had
counted hearths, hadn't
you, those charred,
paper-

thin deposits in which, you'd
tell us, they —yes, they, the very first— first
cupped, incredulous, the
un-

touchable.

~

'cinder,' you'd reported, and,
sometime later,
'psalm,' of you, though, squatting
a-
mongst your
plumb lines, sunlight
shimmering down the blade of your scalpel, knew, in

fact, nothing. knew, for all
our
overloaded circuitry, only
this growing paucity, rarefaction, the lapses that
lay, now, be-

tween one substantive
and an-
other. whole weeks, for

instance, between 'ash,' say, and 'ochre,' the
words themselves as if
wafted, now, on
ever-

more
tenuous
frequencies.  of you, though, of

you sifting
through so much sediment for some
all-
determinate, all-
establishing, evolutionary instant, no,

nearly nothing, now, if
not, yes, 'roses' sometimes, and

sometimes 'wind.' 'twinge,' too, as if some
minor, recurrent, muscular
contraction (a
memento of
sorts) still held you, there in the midst of
all

that stratified
calcination.


        no, had never been further, you'd
told us, never before
come to
measure, as they'd called it, so much
'eloquent vestige.' yes, there, just there, as

your words scattered in the
very
updrafts wherein
words first had, as if hesitatingly, a-

risen.

# TOWARDS THE BLANCHED ALPHABETS

... like so much weather
out of the west, sound arrives with its
scooped
hollows, the caves it makes in the
very midst of

mass. wrapped, now, in the
blanched
half

of antiphon, you're carried in its
quick, irresonant folds, its
mute
repliques. saying only
what you can't, haunting only
what isn't, you drift, now, through the

intervals. there, in those
late
landscapes, that
vaporous ground: grammar's

ultimate retreat. really yours, these
fingers? this breath
dismembered
for the sake of some final reprieve?
spoke, you

wrote, where speech couldn't, spelling
'hand' free
from hand, 'moon'

from its florid marshes. were
what's left, the

air's
least outlines: mask
that's creasing the folds of the face, there,

just there, where the face
had
already vanished.

# *from* BARROCO: AN ESSAY

you, but
you, but the un-
remitting *replicata* of your own

in-
voluted self. moved, didn't you, through the
blown foam of so much
broken

grammar. there, in
those disseminated spaces, was
'thirst,' you
wondered, still a word? a quantity? for
words, once,
were ladders, scaffolds, the props and stays of
their own

ev-
anescent volumes.

                              hold, then, to each
abandoned ellipse; crouch within the
wobbling contours of so much
muffled
e-

laboration. for here, at least, once
happened: heard
it-

self happen. yes, here, just
here, for instance, once hung, polyphonous, a

vaulted dome, and, within, a
bevy of bright,
ray-

shaken stars, modulated on
breath a-
lone. feed, then, on
aftermath. yes, sip, residual, from so much

vacua. for the hollow droplet still
re-
tains, as if
resonant, its very emission. listen, then. yes,
listen. glean from the

silence, silences. and, so doing,
quench yourself on the
emptiness
of

each parched, irreparable
instant.

## LUBERON

only there, in the hills'
deepest creases, would you grow, at
last, legible, hear
your-

self happen in each dark
spark-
hearted foliation.  weren't you, after
all, your very
own antecedent, the organs you'd

bring, mumbling, into that
arena of
leaves, thistles, ledges?  there, that
is, where your breath, at
last, might
en-

counter mass?  wed, then, the interval of
each
articulated
instant, the acorn that

glows, as if epiphanous, at its own
ac-
cording.  for only the pleat,
finally, speaks.  and, in the name of the
neither, resonant,
echoes.

# FRESQUE

. . . nothing
was what their muscles ground at, what they
straddled —momentous— all
buttocks and

breasts within the fastness of that dilapitated
plaster.  wouldn't the scrolled clouds, the
puffed shrubs themselves
draw from that
un-

suckled drop?  teeth, too, and the
utter silence of
all
that exhortation: yes, theirs,
theirs, once again, asking so much more out of
something that,

nebulous, is
never more than that much unremitting naught.

LANGUEDOC

    . . . rolling in gold
    isometric sections, autumn's troughed vineyards
    foam to the
    oaks'

    very edges.   you who'd
    squeeze fire, plumb shadow —no, not for their
    words, but for the words' all-
    but-

    obliterated antecedent— enter, now, into light's
    last
    lingering retreats.   weren't
    'moss,' 'mistletoe,' but notes, once, struck
    off that utterly

    elusive instrument?   viol that set air itself to
    so
    many vibrant particles?   runs, runs now to
    the very fingertips,
    that

    twinge, that thin
    il-
    legible tremor: the sputtering residue, perhaps, of
    a vocable empty, receptive e-

    nough, once, to
    be-
    get.   you who'd listen, who'd hear, who'd
    linger in the wash of

    this spent episode, while cherishing, as you
    did, something
    al-
    together lesser yet.

# CREATION

. . . what if air itself
were little more than the air's
resonant chamber; the
wisteria, in all its knots and pendulosity, but the
vibratory surface of
some al-

together ob-
fuscated creation.  you, cued to
nothing you'd
ever known, register, now, these

bars, measures, *contrappunti*, claiming them for your
very own when, in

fact, they're little more than the
random dictates of
what, in
passing, mistook your body for
instrument and your slightest breath for incantation.

# Itself Wilds

T HE CONSTELLATION OF INNOVATIVE POETIC STRATE-
gies traced in this book is fairly simple to summarize. It begins
with imagistic clarity, a poetics of *contact* that replaces the self-involved
abstraction of a transcendental and immaterial soul with an immediacy
to the material world we inhabit, a Ch'an attention to everyday experi-
ence. This poetic immediacy combines with two formal approaches to or-
ganizing a poem, both rich in philosophical implications. First is organic
poetic form: a language of the body and the natural rhythms of thought.
In its wilder incarnations, this becomes an improvisational poetry of pri-
mal mind operating in spontaneous and selfless freedom. The second
approach, often overlapping with the first, involves techniques of discon-
tinuous fragmentation or collage that open the logical narrative of thought
to non-logical insight and silence. In this, it opens identity beyond the con-
strictive structures of thought and memory, thereby allowing conscious-
ness its most primal and spacious expanse.

These poetic strategies and the philosophical ideas embedded in them
represent the fabric from which the entire range of modern poetry is made.
However conventional or experimental, and however much they embrace
some and not others, virtually all modern poetry takes these strategies
and ideas as operational assumptions. Rather than the voice of a bodi-
less transcendental soul, it speaks in a voice fully embodied and in direct

engagement with material existence. And those philosophical assumptions all involve, most deeply, the weaving together of consciousness and Cosmos; so however much it is a poetry of personal expression, it is also a voice of the Cosmos.

The challenge of the modern American avant-garde, its strategies and ideas, is most fundamentally a challenge to the nature of language itself. Language in the literate West is a mimetic structure in which words refer to things, point to them as if from some transcendental outside realm. This conception of language is embedded in the West's dominant origin myth, the story of Adam created by God as a "soul" already endowed with language. And of course God created the world by speaking commands. The assumption here is that language did not evolve out of natural process, that language is instead a kind of transcendental realm that somehow always existed independently of natural process, that it predates the appearance of humans and indeed the very earth itself. Because mimetic language exists in this myth as an assumption, it is rarely noticed or questioned, even now that the myth itself has been questioned and abandoned. That myth may be discredited, but when language functions in that mimetic sense, as it always does for us, it still embodies an absolute ontological separation between material reality and an immaterial soul. That separation defines the most fundamental level of our experience, and it is exactly what the modern avant-garde challenges.

In a more historical sense, the origins of mimetic language and its transcendental realm can be traced back through the evolution of language. In preliterate oral cultures, language as thought and speech was an organic and fleeting phenomenon integral to all other natural phenomena in the steady unfolding of change. There was no spirit-center conjuring and directing thought, so it was essentially the Cosmos thinking and speaking. But with the advent of writing, thought began to feel like a timeless realm outside the world of change, and this created the sense of being a center of identity separate from natural process. As writing continued to develop its own logic and complexity, thought began more and more to follow its own patterns, patterns that seemed radically different from those of empirical reality. People could write thoughts down, then scrutinize them, revise and rethink them, return to them at some later time and place, all of which established the illusion of language as mimetic—a transcendental realm pointing at empirical reality—and along with that, the illusion of a self-enclosed mental realm free of the strictures of time, an interior into which we withdrew further and further.

Writing began as pictographic, manifesting a direct connection to the empirical world; but with the exception of Chinese, it became alphabetic so as to phonetically represent the sounds of speech. With the rise of alphabetic writing, pictographs were replaced by arrangements of letters: words that have an arbitrary relationship to the things they name. Hence, the pictographic relationship to things themselves was replaced by a relationship to the human voice, adding another dimension to that self-enclosed reflexive relationship to ourselves. This is complicated by the fact that alphabetic writing, by phonetically representing speech sounds, objectifies speech, distancing it as part of an outside world, much as mimetic naming distances empirical reality. And so, consciousness as open and integral to natural process was replaced by an immaterial soul ontologically separate from and outside of material reality. It was only at this point in human cultural development that the biblical origin myth became possible. It must have been a back-creation conjured by a literate culture that had mastered the technology of writing, for only then had mimetic language and its transcendental spirit-realm come into existence, only then had we come to see ourselves as timeless souls unaffected by the constant process of change, spirit-centers peering out at an alien and transitory world.

What the modern avant-garde was reaching toward, at a level so fundamental it was perhaps never quite seen, was a non-mimetic language that would free consciousness of that self-enclosed distancing from reality. Non-mimetic language is the language of oral cultures before the advent of writing. It shaped consciousness in those primal cultures, which is why so many avant-garde poets were interested in the primitive, even if they never quite saw it at this foundational level. To reimagine experience at this level is essentially a meditative mind-experiment. In our everyday lives we see the world as an assemblage of independent facts, each of which has a name. If you empty the mind of all thought and idea, all assumption and belief, empty it of names and finally of language with its mimetic function, you encounter a very different empirical reality. Rather than an assemblage of things, it appears as a single tissue. That tissue is only divided into individual things when we name them. But seen with the clarity of an empty primal mind, it is clear that those names emerge from the undifferentiated tissue exactly like the things they name, and at exactly the same moment: it is only when the word *tree* emerges that the tree itself emerges as an independent entity in the field of existence. The tree itself exists prior to the naming, of course, but it isn't separated out as an independent entity. So in non-mimetic language a word is associated with a thing not because of a mimetic "pointing" at the thing, but because it shares that thing's embryonic source.

Non-mimetic language assumes that primal generative cosmology we have encountered many times in this book, and the more primal and accurate experience of time inherent to that cosmology. Not linear, the familiar metaphysical river flowing past, or even cyclical—as time in primal cultures is imprecisely described—it is an all-encompassing generative now, a constant burgeoning forth in which the ten thousand things emerge from the generative source-tissue of existence and return to that same source. Only in this experience of reality as an all-encompassing emergent present can that non-mimetic language exist. Each time the word *tree* is uttered, the word and the tree itself emerge together into existence at that origin-moment. And this makes the language act (thought or speech) a wondrous thing, for it moves always at that generative origin-moment, each instant a small miracle of creation where word and thing come into existence simultaneously. And so, as we have seen, non-mimetic language free of a transcendental spirit-center could be described as earth thinking itself through us.

Remarkably, this account of non-mimetic language also describes our everyday experience of language. Close observation reveals that everyday speech, thought, and even writing occurs without that "interference of the individual as ego." There is no ego directing the process. Instead, the process is simply happening (*emerging*, as the primal generative cosmology would describe it), exactly like thought or speech in oral cultures. That spirit-center only appears when we step back and describe what is happening: *I spoke. I thought. I wrote.* We assume that "I" to be a transcendental spirit-center, even if we deny it philosophically, for in fact our language itself assumes it. So in a sense, the spiritual practice shared across the modern avant-garde project is an attempt to return us not just to immediate experience, but also to the true nature of everyday speech, thought, and writing.

Although ancient Chinese culture was intensely literate, classical Chinese was in its deepest nature primal and non-mimetic. The technology of writing should have created that mimetic distancing of a spirit-center from the empirical, but the primal non-mimetic structure seems to have survived in classical Chinese from the earliest levels of Paleolithic proto-Chinese cultures. There are two reasons for this. First, Chinese never gave up the pictographic for the alphabetic. However much it was complicated by phonetic elements, ideograms preserved that direct connection to things themselves, and that connection was a primal non-mimetic one: words as images of things, sharing with them their origins and essential natures. And second, there is virtually no grammar in classical Chinese, so the meaning of each word must be drawn out of empty grammatical space, as if you were drawing it out of a primal mystery of origins. In this, the language maintains that non-mimetic structure wherein words emerge from a kind of origin place shared by the things they name. Because of these two unique characteristics—pictographic words and minimal grammar—classical Chinese operates in that primal cosmology of an ongoing generative now. And indeed, there are no verb tenses in classical Chinese, so the language operates always in that all-encompassing present.

When it is shaped by non-mimetic language and a generative cosmology, consciousness possesses that primal immediacy the avant-garde aspired to. Since Chinese is the only literate culture in which this immediacy survived, it makes sense that is where the avant-garde, operating in its own highly literate culture, would find access to it. Fenollosa recognized this primitive dimension in Chinese language and poetry—if only vaguely—and what he didn't recognize in his essay was transported beneath the surface to the avant-garde poets who followed. Combining modern anthropological knowledge about the origins of language with his intuited sense of the non-mimetic dimensions of Chinese, he proposed a return of language and thought to that primal moment where language emerged out of natural process, a moment revealing language's true non-mimetic nature. He said "the prehistoric poets who created language discovered the whole harmonious framework of nature," and he described those poets building "accumulations of metaphor into structures of language and into systems of thought."

Here Fenollosa is reaching toward a non-mimetic oral-culture language integral to the verbal nature of reality, a language that entails no transcendental spirit-center. This is what, without ever quite realizing it, the philosophical thrust of the poetic avant-garde was aspiring to. Its challenge to the Western spirit-center is most fundamentally a challenge to the mimetic nature of language, and it is why the poets all problematize and transform language in some way: Imagism, ideogrammic method, primal orality, improvisational spontaneity, associative leaps, organic form, egoless composition, fragmentation, collage. Whatever form these poetic strategies take, they are most fundamentally attempts to get beyond the mimetic structure of language, however little the practitioners recognized it. And no matter how hard they tried, there was no eluding the mimetic nature of English.

This is the unrecognized conflict driving the modern avant-garde. What they most fundamentally wanted was a primal non-mimetic language where there is no soul experiencing life from a kind of transcendental outside. But because their language can only operate mimetically, this remains forever impossible—so the poets invented radical strategies capable of somehow approaching that primal state. In this, theirs are poems lit up by an inevitable and ongoing failure, poems in which this failure generates one revelatory success after another. Each of these successes brings us a little closer to inhabiting the world at a wild depth and primal immediacy where identity is integral to earth—that dwelling in which our thought is earth thinking itself through us—where *who we are* is *where we are*. And in this dwelling, *where we are* becomes our deepest and most personal song,

song the title of which begins where memory leaves off,

song the title of which opens a place for whatever occurs next,

song the title of which is thrust up into ridgelines, glacier-scoured, veined with streams and rivers, and fading to blue in the distance,

song the title of which exhausts the blessing between each breath and the next,

song the title of which ripples shimmering in a stream flowing above its shadow in sand,

song the title of which asks in the eyes of a starved child gazing
at her starved father,

song the title of which flurries in snow falling through the beauty
of falling snow,

song the title of which breathes through empty skies,

song the title of which is the difference between loneliness in
summer and loneliness littered with autumn,

song the title of which opens a place for the stars,

song the title of which ends before the earliest name of silence,

song the title of which occurrence scatters always into its own directions,

song the title of which is somewhere near you, something unborn
and always beginning just now:

# CREDITS

EZRA POUND: "In a Station of the Metro," "The River-Merchant's Wife: A Letter," "The Jewel Stairs' Grievance," "Separation on the River Kiang" from *Personae: Collected Shorter Poems.* Copyright 1926. Reprinted by permission of New Directions Publishing. *The Chinese Written Character as a Medium for Poetry.* Copyright 1936. Reprinted by permission of City Lights Publishing.

WILLIAM CARLOS WILLIAMS: " The Red Wheelbarrow," "The Locust Tree in Flower," "The Locust Tree in Flower," "To a Poor Old Woman," "Summer Song," "The Right of Way," "The Wildflower," "Poem," "Between Walls," "Fine Work with Pitch and Copper," "Young Woman at a Window," "Autumn," "Breakfast" from *The Collected Earlier Poems.* Copyright 1951. Reprinted by permission of New Directions Publishing. "Picture of a Nude in a Machine Shop," "Suzanne" from *The Collected Later Poems.* Copyright 1962. Reprinted by permission of New Directions Publishing.

ROBINSON JEFFERS: "Natural Music," "November Surf," "Gray Weather," "New Mexican Mountain," "October Week-End" from *The Collected Poetry of Robinson Jeffers.* Copyright 1988. Reprinted by permission of Stanford University Press. "Continent's End," "Rock and Hawk," "Love the Wild Swan," "Hurt Hawks," "The Eye," "Carmel Point," "The Deer Lay Down Their Bones" from *The Selected Poetry of Robinson Jeffers.* Copyright 1938. Reprinted by permission of Random House Publishing.

KENNETH REXROTH: "New Moon," "A Restless Night in Camp" from *One Hundred Poems from the Chinese.* Copyright 1956. Reprinted by permission